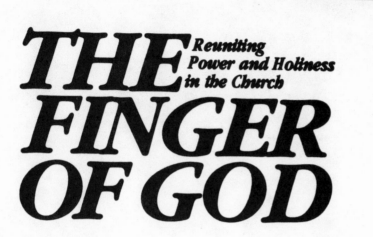

THE FINGER OF GOD

Reuniting
Power and Holiness
in the Church

THE FINGER OF GOD

Reuniting Power and Holiness in the Church

MARK RUTLAND

BRISTOL BOOKS
WILMORE, KY 40390

Library of Congress Card Number: 88-71098
ISBN: 0-917851-24-2
Suggested Subject Headings:
1. Church Renewal
2. Holiness
Recommended Dewey Decimal Classification: 262.0017

BRISTOL BOOKS
An imprint of Good News, Forum for Scriptural Christianity, Inc.
308 East Main Street • Wilmore, Kentucky 40390

CONTENTS

A Divorce and a Wedding

❖

TIME TO REUNITE HOLINESS AND POWER

Only a few years ago at a small holiness college in the Midwest, the body of a student, gruesomely mutilated, was found in his room. The county coroner sealed off the blood-drenched dormitory room as a crime scene. To her it appeared an obvious and brutal homicide. Yet the local Methodist pastor quietly but steadfastly maintained it was suicide.

"Suicide?" the coroner asked. "How can a boy inflict dozens of savage wounds on himself? He would have passed out. College suicides take poison," she continued, "they don't slaughter themselves with a butcher knife."

But she was wrong. The forensic tests, fingerprints and detailed inquest proved conclusively that it was indeed a suicide!

After the inquest the coroner visited the pastor at his home. "You knew this was a suicide," she said. "How could a boy do that?"

The pastor explained that if a person's obsessive drive for perfection is met by deep disappointment, self-hatred—blind, vicious, *lethal*—can be the result. The boy was killing his worst enemy because he could not measure up to some internal standard of legal holiness.

What had the boy done? Who knows. Maybe an impure thought had darted across his brain. Perhaps some immature habit continued to dog him. Perhaps it was some outright sin. That is hardly important. The boy is dead, and his family grieves in confusion.

Meanwhile, just a few states away, a multimillion-dollar televangelism empire crumbles around the slumped shoulders of its fallen hero. The Christian community watches in horrified dismay as the whole grimy story unfolds like a Harold Robbins novel. Sexual indecency, rolex watches, million-dollar salaries, expensive homes and air-conditioned dog houses make a laughingstock of evangelical Christianity in general and the charismatic renewal in particular.

A guilt-ridden holiness college boy takes his life and a glitzy, Hollywood-style Pentecostal preacher falls into materialism and gross immorality. What can these two desperate tragedies possibly have in common?

Historically in the Church an emphasis on the work, person and ministry of the Holy Spirit has always been concomitant with renewal. The Holy Spirit *is* the Spirit of revival.

The anointing of the Holy Spirit for *power in ministry* is axiomatic. Furthermore his work of *sanctification* in the believer is a fundamental biblical doctrine. Both emphases find their roots in Scripture to be sure and both are valid. The problem is that in the heat of revival, many have been receptive to either *power in ministry* or *holiness of life* to the exclusion or even denial of the other.

The strange and perplexing historical reality is that the "theological schools" which have encamped around these poles of *power* and *holiness* have frequently seen themselves as adversaries. Their spiritual, historical and biblical connection has sometimes been obvious to everyone but themselves. They have often presented the tragi-comic picture of Siamese twins in a fistfight.

Who is Who?

Churches such as the Nazarene, Wesleyan, Salvation Army and Christian Missionary Alliance and portions of the United Methodist Church have become known as "holiness" denominations. The Assemblies of God, Church of God, Pentecostal Holiness and (since the 60s) the charismatics have assumed the role of "Pentecostal" denominations with an emphasis on gifts and ministry.

Even such a wry observer as the *New York Times* has seen the connection. In its February 23, 1988 edition writer Peter Steinfels describes the Assemblies of God:

> The denomination's roots are in what is called the "Holiness Revival," a wave of religious fervor that swept through the ranks of American Methodists in the decades after the Civil War.
>
> The movement expressed a rigorous quest for personal Christian perfection, a traditional Methodist concern that the "holiness" adherents believed to have been attentuated as Methodist churches became more sedate and middle class.
>
> Church members also looked for a "second blessing" by the Holy Spirit that marked their sanctification. One strand of the holiness movement became known as Pentecostals for their belief that all Christians should seek the same gifts of the Holy Spirit, including speaking in "tongues," that Jesus' disciples received on what Christian churches celebrate as the feast of Pentecost.

Today, groups emphasizing these gifts—or charisms—of the Spirit form charismatic movements within almost every major branch of Christianity.

Throughout the history of the Church, especially in the West, these two divergent streams of renewal have repeatedly evidenced themselves. At times they have appeared to flow together for a season only to separate again in angry turbulence. At other times both seemed to vanish, leaving less hope than a sun-baked creek bed in a summer drought. Still more confusing were those periods when they seemed to suddenly, mysteriously change places, directions and expressions.

There have been times when the sober "holiness movement" has found voice for shouts of victory, has been "slain in the Spirit" and has gained strength to run and leap in the aisles. The Pentecostals have frequently been more legalistic and bound-up in holiness rules than their "holiness" cousins. Then the charismatics exploded onto the scene in the 60s as exciting, excitable, delighted, delightful, exasperating love-children. Both of the embarrassed probable-parents fervently denied paternity.

The Need for a Wedding

My burden in this book is to give expression to a long-held dream of mine. If the deep, solid theological roots of the holiness movement could be wedded to the liberty and dancing joy of the Pentecostal-charismatic experience the result might well be a new Great Awakening.

The sins, excesses and theological absurdities allowed by the Charismatics must now be met with balanced biblical doctrine. The holiness movement has often been so theologically "proper" that it is certainly right—*dead* right. It badly needs the vitality of the Pentecostals.

This book is about a wedding. The marriage of holiness and power in the kingdom of God. The second half of the book speaks to some practical applications of all that a marriage made in heaven might mean. These include evangelism, the gifts, worship, order and healing.

A precious friend, upon reading the manuscript, said, "I believe this is a fair book. You have equally insulted both groups."

I pray that, somehow, it will not be received that way. My dream is that some readers will say "Yes, yes—that's it! We Pentecostals and Charismatics *need* a new and exciting emphasis on holiness." Perhaps others may say, "It's true! It's really true. We holiness folks *need* the power of ministry in the kingdom and we need it now."

God's Holiness, God's Power

CHAPTER I

The Cosmic Switchboard

❖

THE NATURE OF GOD'S HOLINESS

*I*f the charismatic movement is to mean any more to the modern church than momentary pyrotechnics it must eschew the sensational and lay hold of the substantial. No doubt the miracle wind of God's Spirit is moving in exciting ways. Yet where the heart of the movement is not sanctified, its ministries devoted to healing and power fall prey to brokenness and fleshy impotence.

By the same token, the great Wesleyan holiness school is in danger of becoming hardly more than a lot of blustery old men rattling rusty sabers and shouting antiquated camp meeting slogans to no one but themselves. Holiness is not served by iron-clad, pharisaical legalists campaigning more for a depression-era vocabulary rather than for true revival.

A great revival can still belong to this generation. If, that is, it is not forfeited by peevish preachers more intent on defending the sacred cows of their own private theological stockyards than upon seeing an unhindered move of God.

"Great is the Lord, and most worthy of praise, in the city of our God, his holy mountain" (Psalm 48:1).

The kingdom of God is a kingdom of holiness because our God is a God of holiness. The kingdom is like unto the King. We must again invest ourselves creatively in uncovering the great hope of humanity, which is the holiness of God.

Scripture affords no lovelier divine description than holiness. For a needy, neurotic humanity longing for some faint ray of hope that God is after all *good*, this one word *holiness* affords a splendid munificence. It is pregnant with hope, pungent with meaning and plenteous in mercy. And yet it remains veiled in mystery and discarded in contempt.

Driving through a small town in North Georgia I spied a rudely hand-painted sign with an arrow underneath the words: "Holey Ghost Revival."

Perhaps, I thought, *the blockade to true revival in the church lies more in the spelling than I had imagined.* Holiness, properly spelled, is essentially a matter of wholeness. To be holy is to be perfect—that is, by definition that which is holy is neither lacking nor burdened with the superfluous.

A "perfect" circle is one defined by being equidistant from the center at every point on the perimeter. Such a circle could, in a sense, be said to be "holy." It meets the definition of perfect, undiluted "circleness." Now, a circle lacking even one degree of enclosure is more "holey" than holy. By the same token if that same gap on the perimeter were to be "filled in" with a line inconsistent with the definition, the circle, though complete in one way, remains profoundly imperfect. It is now an "unholy" circle.

A lady in one church said, "Brother Mark, you keep talking about "drawing nigh unto." I don't want to get close to God. I just want to get over in a corner and sneak into heaven quietly. I don't want to be a saint. I just don't want to go to hell."

"I cannot believe what I'm hearing!" I exclaimed.

"I can explain it easily," she said calmly. "When I started the ninth grade I set my heart on finishing high school with straight C's. And I did. You see, if you fail you have to repeat, and I wanted *out*. But if you start making A's people begin to expect things of you.

"It's exactly like that with God," she continued. "If you're too bad you'll go to hell, and I don't want that. But if you're too good, he'll send you to India, and I don't want that either."

Quite apart from the obvious theology of works, her theory of "C-class Christianity" betrayed a pathetically distorted understanding of the character and nature of God. Her confusion, far more serious than the merely epidural misjudgment of "how God acts," sprang from her twisted concept of "who God is."

Far from being an isolated story, hers is a tragedy repeated with only slight variations in the lives of multiplied millions of sincere, but sincerely confused, Christians. These crippled children of a God who is whole live shadowy lives of terror, fearful of a God they do not know and longing for a father they can trust. Without knowledge of the holiness of God, these people will—if they do not perish—at least huddle in cold darkness away from the light of his marvelous love.

The Question of Who God Is

Out of the burning bush God spoke to Moses, calling him to the great life's work for which he had been raised up. It was a task of monumental proportion and must have been stunning to Moses. Of even greater significance to the individual believer is Jehovah's self-declaration in that same conversation.

"Moses said to God, 'Suppose I go to the Israelites and say to them, "The God of your fathers has sent me to you," and they ask me, "What is his name?" Then what shall I tell them?'" (Ex. 3:13). It is quite provocative to note that Moses required no such revelation to sway the might of Egypt. The demonstration of power was sufficient there. This message was for the bound and backslidden people of God who needed fresh revelation. The children of Israel had been so long in slavery amidst the pantheistic paganism of Egypt that they had lost sight of the true nature of the true God.

"We know the name of Isis and the name of Ra," Moses could imagine their responding. "When you speak of the God of our fathers, what is his name?"

"Now Lord," Moses seems to be saying to God in a peculiarly earthy bit of wisdom. "These are a people with more than four hundred years of theological confusion bred into them. They have largely forgotten your name *and* who you are. I am *not* going down there and tell them a burning bush sent me! What is your name?"

Moses appears to grasp the principle that the kind of genuine, obedient faith necessary to spring open a revival (another name for deliverance from bondage) will not be found in an atmosphere of confusion. In fact, it is upon that very principle that Moses appeals to God for a fresh revelation.

God's declaration of his own holiness is magnificent! "No more," he seems to say to Moses, "shall my people be in bondage to distorted images of me. I am that I am."

We are free in the unshakable knowledge that God is nothing other, less or more than himself. The present tense, unchanging, unchangeable ultimate reality of the universe, the ground of all truth and the hope of humanity, is that God is perfectly God.

In the Far East an old woman told me of an odd custom surrounding the birth of a baby. If the child were perfect, healthy and of the desired sex it would be immediately hidden. The father would plunge hysterically out of his house loudly cursing the gods with all the appropriate histrionics. Screaming as if in agony of soul and renting his garments like some half-mad, Old Testament monarch he would revile the gods with blasphemous epithets.

Similarly, when visitors arrived to view the new baby, knowing glances and silent winks of congratulations would be exchanged, but howls of indignation would be lofted heavenward.

"Curses, O curses on all the gods," they would wail, "for the grief brought on this poor home. This wretched, pitiful excuse for a baby will bring no happiness to this home!"

Bizarre? Certainly! But it is the predictable end of theological confusion. You see, in their view the gods were simply human beings whose power had been multiplied by thousands. One normal human brain thus magnified becomes a formidable force and one to be reckoned with. The problem is that if the gods are simply "overgrown human beings" their human frailties, weaknesses, lusts and sins are necessarily magnified as well!

Hence the gods become petty, selfish, whimsical demon-spirits to be pacified but hardly to be adored. If such gods saw the joy of a young couple nestling its newborn progeny, they might in envious pique maim or even kill the child.

Only slightly more sophisticated is the blithe Greek acceptance of a god who in rapacious lust would assume animal form for the bestial molestation of mortal woman. These primitive but more subtle forms of this same heresy are hardly to be avoided if God is seen as the unpredictable but powerful ruler of the universe.

Can God Do Anything?

As an undergraduate student I was confronted on my Christian faith by an atheistic professor. He was one of those militant, aggressive atheists not content to simply go to hell. He wanted all the rest of us to go with him.

"Rutland," he said to me in class one day, "I understand you're a Christian." He spoke the word "Christian" as one might say "fascist," "nazi" or "cat-hater."

"Yes, Dr. Johnson [not his real name]," I said, "I am."

"Then you must believe in God," he concluded.

"Yes, of course," I said, "one can hardly be a Christian without believing in God."

"Well," he said, "let me ask you this. Can your God do everything?"

"Oh, yes," I answered, eager to make a profession of faith before him and the whole class. Alas, mine was an answer drenched in hopeless naiveté.

"Then riddle me this," he said, with a triumphant verbal lunge, "Can he make a rock he cannot pick up?"

The professor smiled wickedly, as if to say, "touché," and gloated over the spectacle of yet another hapless Christian impaled on his pet pattern of thrust, parry, thrust. At that point there *was* no answer.

Ah, but how often I have considered returning to college with what I know *now*. I wonder if he is still asking that same question.

More than perhaps he even realized, this is the greatest question of all. And it demands a bold answer; yet one informed with true biblical faith.

Can God do everything?

NO! Praise his name, God cannot do everything. Because he is holy he cannot sin, lie, cheat, steal or treat us falsely. He cannot will, think, act or speak in opposition to his own nature. He cannot contradict himself. He is I AM, and he must in every moment *be* I AM. No, God *cannot* do everything!

Unlimited in power, God is more surely bound than a galley slave. He can never be less than nor other than who he is. He must always be true, perfect, holy "Godness." Hence his every impulse, motive and deed find reality only within the circumscribed parameters of his own nature. Simply put, God cannot, even for a fraction of a second, quit being God.

God—An Angry Heavenly Cop?

But it is not God's holiness that separates me from God. It is *my* sin. In fact, it is only because God *is* holy that I can draw nigh unto him in faith, knowing that he is to me, no less than he is to anyone else in all the earth, I AM.

There is not a god of the river, a god of the sea or a god of fire. Neither is there a god for plumbers, one for electricians and one for seminary professors. "Hear, O Israel, the Lord your God is *one God*; and he is the same yesterday, today and forever" (Deuteronomy 6:4, italics mine).

Furthermore, he is the same in character in all three persons. Because God is holy, when he breathes, he breathes himself. When he speaks, his Word is himself. Whether he is the *God-head*, the pre-existent Word, the *Word* in expressed form, or *breath* he is not variable in nature.

"In the beginning was the Word, and the Word was with God, and the Word was God. He was with God in the beginning" (John 1:1-2).

I once had a great friend whom I loved dearly. Barry (a pseudonym) was a fine tennis player as well as a warm and witty companion. His wife, Martha, however (the name is changed to protect the guilty), was demonized. She was as mean-hearted, mean-spirited and cold-blooded a woman as ever lived.

Martha refused to condescend to such trite niceties as answering the phone with a "hello," "good morning" or even "Barry and Martha's." Instead she would jerk the phone from its cradle as if personally insulted by its ring and loudly demand "What?!" in a tone that would have evoked envy in a gestapo agent.

"Martha," I would say, "this is Mark Rutland. Is Barry home?" "Yes," she would snip. "He's home, but you can't speak to him. I'm tired of his dead-beat tennis-bum friends calling up every time he has a few hours off. He's not going to play tennis *today*. We're going to work here at the house, and *anyway*, why don't you get married and settle down?"

This had a decided tendency to ruin my day. I finally became Unwilling to risk such harrowing encounters.

"Barry," I told my friend, "I love you and want to play tennis. But from now on *you* call *me*. My mama answers the phone with 'Hello.'"

If I could have secreted myself across the street to watch the house until Martha left, I might have called. But I would rather have missed the tennis date with my friend than risk hearing her shout "What?!" into the phone.

God himself alone knows how many multiplied millions of serious, church-trained Christian folks are utterly paralyzed in their devotional access to God because they are not certain who will answer the phone when they dial heaven. If they could be certain to get Jesus on the main line they would perhaps approach prayer with confidence. They perceive God the Father to be an angry heavenly cop. God the Holy Spirit is often hidden behind an almost impregnable insulation of ignorance and prejudice.

A great many mainline Christians, while espousing Trinitarianism, are actually functioning Unitarians, serving the God Jesus and living in unwholeness and uninformed terror of the full Godhead. This heresy is cultivated and encouraged unthinkingly at a cultural level through much of accepted worship practice.

The Pocahontas Heresy

I have childhood memories of schizophrenic Sundays that schooled me in the worship of a schizophrenic God. Sunday school was gay and warm. A smiling, gray-haired teacher condescended to sit on a chair my size. She colored pictures with me and told me that Jesus loved me. How easy it was to believe! His blue-eyed, chestnut-haired countenance beautified the classroom wall, and upon our felt-board the teacher fearlessly put children right on Jesus' lap. We celebrated Jesus' love for little children in general and for us personally with every song. At Easter the soft, warm bunny our teacher brought in a pasteboard carton seemed to have some vague connection to this misty-eyed Jesus and his love for children.

But church, now *that* was a different matter! The winding

staircase up from the basement Sunday school classrooms led distinctly *away* from the festive presence of Jesus. Adults do not take seriously the culture-shock experienced by a child who leaves his mother-like teacher singing "Jesus Loves Me" to the lively accompaniment of an ancient upright piano, and enters a somber oaken sanctuary with an organist hunched like the phantom of the opera belting Bach's Toccata in D-minor. Every kid knows that something is spooky about a place they don't allow babies. Then out comes the preacher in a long black dress. The choir pompously parades in wearing nightgowns. Gone is the friendly smile of the Sunday school teacher. Now the pastor, looking for all the world like a buzzard with a glandular problem, drones with funereal intonations that, "Gawd is in his holy temple, let all the earth keep SILENCE before him." Jesus is hardly mentioned again in this place, only "Gawd"!

This is hardly a setting designed to draw a child to the bosom of the Father. It may more nearly scare the wits out of him. And what does it say about the Trinity? That part of God (the good part, the Sunday school part) called Jesus seems to be on *my* side. God the Father is obviously angry at the whole universe. And the Holy Spirit seems to be only window dressing, used in baptisms, communion and monotonous, meaningless creeds. For how many contemporary church-goers has it become a case of Father, Son and What's-His-Name?

The result of all this is a particularly noxious and subtle blasphemy that often passes for evangelical preaching. I call it "Pocahontas Theology" in honor of that maiden who threw herself sacrificially across Capt. John Smith, thus saving him from her murderous father.

Repugnant to the gospel is that horrifying heresy which implies that Jesus was, like Pocahontas, saving humanity from God. "That God was reconciling the world to himself in Christ, not counting men's sins against them. And he has committed to us the message of reconciliation" (2 Cor. 5:19). "This is love: not that we loved God, but that he loved us and sent his Son as an atoning sacrifice for our sins" (1 John 4:10). "For God so loved the world that he gave his one and only Son, that whoever believes in him shall not perish but have eternal life. For God did not send his Son into the world to condemn the world, but to save the world through him" (John 3:16-17).

The great hope of humanity is the holiness of God. On the cross, Jesus was not saving us from the holiness of God. Hardly! He was proving it! The cross is a window on the soul of God. Calvary was not the world's idea. Jesus is called the "Lamb that was slain from the creation of the world" (Lev. 13:8). In the sacrifice on Calvary, I AM died for humanity, the creatures' sin. God is perfect personhood. He must not be less than perfect in all three persons. I AM is always I AM. How can I AM be other or less than *he was*? Unthinkable. He is in all three persons true to his own unchanging, unchangeable, ultimate, perfect holiness.

What Is God Like?

Now, if God is always the same, one question must be answered immediately. What is God, always, in all three persons, *like*?

The answer afforded by 1 John 4:8 is marvelous indeed, and magnificent in its simplicity. "*God is love.*"

God is I AM, is holiness, is love.

That simple statement is in itself a three-in-one. The whole and its three parts are proper entities. God is I AM. I AM is holiness. Holiness is love. God is love!

"I'm no theologian," a certain radio preacher once began. "I'm just a country preacher."

In the light of the confused sermon which followed, one was forced to agree. The Christian, lay or ordained, *must* be a theologian. Theology is quite simply what one believes to be true about God. It is my experience that those who claim not to be theologians are usually just bad ones.

If a woman sees God as an angry, demanding, impossible-to-please step-father-in-the-sky, her "Christianity" will reflect a sadly bound-up, neurotic perfectionism. The God of the nominal Christian businessperson is the distant, insensitive, absentee-landlord to whom homage must be paid twice a year. His or her "religion" will be a reflection of a "nursing-home-God," a doddering, yet respected, senile old man who demands little, offers less and is satisfied with a check and a visit now and then.

The God of holiness, however, so far transcends such pitiful concepts as to make them laughable if they were not so sad. To simply say "God is love" is quite insufficient unless that affirmation is received personally in the light of a biblical concept of God.

"God is love" must be translated, "God is I AM"; God is love in *my* life. "God is love" thus becomes "God loves *me*." I know that he does because God acts, wills speaks and emotes consistently with his own nature. Therefore his will for *me* must be good because he is good. His Word must be true in my life because he is truth. He must love *me* because he is love.

It is not, as one contemporary speaker said, that there is "something about me that turns God on." No! That is tenuous ground for a relationship indeed. What if that which is fetching to God today were to be gone tomorrow?

What if God loves me because I am kind, gentle and loving? That is all well and good until I shout at my kids on the way to Sunday school. The God who was "turned on" by my sweet disposition is now perhaps put off by my ugly impatience.

No! That is the spirit that says today God loves me because I have been good, looked good, served well, preached with an anointing, prayed properly or washed the car. The negative result of such thinking is, all too often, that God is as fickle as I am, his emotions as undependable as ours and his love hardly more sure.

There is nothing I can do to make God love me more. I cannot pray enough, get sanctified enough, win enough people to Jesus or be clever enough to make God love me more. How can I hope by my actions to make perfect love more perfect?

By the same token I cannot make God love me any less. I

cannot sin enough, hate enough or even deny God enough to
make perfect love love me less!

More Than Crumbs Under the Table

If God is I AM and I AM is perfect love then God is perfect
love to *me*. That is the key. We must see that God's love *me-
ward* is magnificently *personal*. God's holiness is not just a force
field of sterile, laboratory cleanness somewhere over the rain-
bow. Perfect love is I AM to *me*. I am never in the corner of his
affections. I am never forgotten, never in the suburbs of his love
and never, ever is he too busy for me.

I am his only project. I am in the center of his heart. I am the
apple of his eye. All of the creative faculties that spoke light into
existence are now fastened, without distraction, wholly on me.

The miracle of God's love is decidedly *not* that there is
enough for the whole human race. That "crumbs under the table"
theology says that God's love is so huge that every man everywhere can get a little. That little crumb, of course, being so
wonderful is quite sufficient. No, no, no! That makes God sound
like an old woman at a USO club trying to stretch the last of the
agape mayonnaise to make sandwiches for all the hungry soldiers.

The miracle of God's love is not that there is enough for us
all to receive a crumb. The miracle is that we each receive it all.
That is *omnipresence*. That God is everywhere does not mean
that a little of him is in all places but that *all* of him is everywhere.

So it is with his love. It is not so much that God has enough
love to go around. It is rather that I am the very object of affection of the great God Jehovah. God does not merely have enough
love for all of us. He loves each of us with all he is, because he
can never be a partial God to anyone.

If we could only understand this one truth, how it would set
us free. We would never again labor to earn the love of God. We

would never again experience those deep depressions and fears that our sins or emotional lows have somehow changed God. How liberated is the believer whose God never changes!

Tying Up the Cosmic Switchboard

How profoundly such basic liberty would change everything about us. For example, many erroneous views of prayer would dissolve immediately. One such view extremely common among even the most serious church folks is what I call the Cosmic Switchboard Theology of prayer.

In this concept God is seen as the harried operator of an absurdly gigantic switchboard in the sky. A corresponding light for each of earth's four and one-half billion occupants demands attention as they pray. Hence God is seen frantically juggling cords between flickering lights. He can manage it most of the time. He is after all God, isn't he?

Now few believers, if any, *formally* verbalize such a distorted view of prayer. Yet I am convinced that millions labor with exactly such a theology at the functional level.

The result is the pitiful little lady in a healing service who refuses to seek prayer for her arthritic fingers because "it's such a little thing and there are so many in worse shape."

What is she afraid of? Perhaps it is that she will tie up the switchboard at the exact moment that someone with terminal cancer is trying to get through. If, however, I know that God is I AM to me, I see that mine is the only light on the board.

A right view of the holiness of God is the basis of all true theology. Once I settle that God is perfect love, I am free to seek him as never before. The neurotic terror of a whimsical and demanding God who cannot be pleased is banished. In its place shines the blinding beauty of holy love that will not let me go.

An elderly woman in a holiness camp meeting wept almost uncontrollably when she realized that the very holiness of God which she feared and very nearly hated was in fact the assurance that God loved her.

"O, God," she sobbed in my arms. "My whole life I ached to make God love me. Just for one day I wanted to feel absolutely acceptable to God. But every time I screamed at my kids or felt too tired to go to church on Wednesday night, I knew I couldn't quite measure up."

Dear, God, forgive us! How many sweet old ladies who have cut their teeth on holiness teaching have broken their own hearts trying to please a God they never really knew? What a tragedy!

God's holiness is the hope of humanity. It is what makes the gospel good news and not bad news. I am not afraid of the holiness of God. It makes me long to draw nigh with faith. It makes me know that despite my frailties, weaknesses, failings and sins, I AM loves *me* because he is holy.

CHAPTER 11

Jason and the Magic Lute

❖

True and False Holiness for the Believer

"I don't have the money," I whispered discreetly to my little daughter Emily. The bicycle she wanted was just a little beyond our reach at that time. "I know you want the bike, Honey, but I just don't have the money now."

"Oh, don't worry, Daddy," she comforted me sweetly. "Just write a check, like Mommy does."

The proposition out of which one approaches any basic question determines an entire set of direct and indirect answers. If one believes that writing a check is a substitute for money, one's final solution arises out of that basic presupposition. The sheriff's department, on the other hand, may well be operating on the fundamental assumption that one's ability to write a check is determined by the actual cash on deposit. Thereby, of course, hangs the tale *and* many a jail term.

By the same token, one's basic view of the nature of God

predetermines one's approach to ethical holiness. How one thinks about God determines the way one understands behavior as an expression of holiness.

It is one thing to talk about the holiness of God in terms of a nature of perfect love, as in the previous chapter. That approach is hardly ever debated. The problem, however, arises as to how holiness is translated into behavior.

Injudicious voices within the classical holiness camp have all too often seemed to be speaking out of a topside-down understanding of the relationship between *nature* and *action*. The basic question is this:

(1) Does nature determine behavior *or*

(2) Does altered behavior change nature.

Consider the two following propositions carefully. They may seem similar but the gulf between them is fixed, and the difference is of monumental significance. Proposition one: God is holy because he does not sin. Holiness here is mere deed. God is being moral in action. A suggested picture is of God possessing some kind of *God Manual* and by exertion of divine willpower he is "obeying the rules." One can only imagine God—shoulder-to-the-wheel, nose-to-the-grindstone— earnestly resisting whatever temptations may come to a being in his position. The likelihood is quite good that he will go on "obeying all the God-rules."

Theological despair is written into this proposition. If God is holy because he does not sin, then he would, by definition, be unholy if he ever did sin. The likelihood may legitimately be reckoned remote, but the possibility is necessary to the integrity of the proposition. If holiness is defined by action, unholiness is also defined by action.

If God is holy because *he does not sin*, the monstrous possibility of his actually sinning hangs over the head of humanity like the sword of Damocles. One split second of God-sin plunges the universe past redemption back into the abyss.

Proposition two: God cannot sin because he is holy. Here holiness is a matter of *nature* with deed the result not the definition. Because God is I AM, sin is simply *defined out.* God is not resisting sin any more than he is striving to do good. Because God is always the Divine Self, he simply acts, does, wills and speaks himself. God fulfills his own nature with the very breath of his nostrils.

This proposition tears holiness out of the clutches of legalism by placing the initial emphasis on "God's heart" (if I may use the term). By no means should this be seen as holding unimportant "what God does." It is instead to say that all thoughts of God's holiness should begin with *who God is* not what God does.

At a cursory examination, making much of the difference between these two propositions seems a classic case of straining at gnats. This issue is no subtle academic point. One's development of a personal theology of such Christian basics as the Holy Spirit, healing, sanctification and prayer spring directly from the fountainhead of one's concept of God's holiness. It is impossible to overstate the ramifications of misunderstanding at this point.

For example, if God is holy because he does not sin, then holiness of life for the believer is a matter of "not sinning." Yet if God does not sin *because he is holy*, then the believer's life of holiness springs more from the concept of a pure heart than from dogged adherence to the rules. The way that I understand God's holiness determines the way I receive his Word, "Be holy because I, the Lord your God, am holy" (Lev. 19:2).

The Don'ts of the Holiness Movement

If this distinction had been more carefully safeguarded in the classical holiness movement much error could have been avoided and perhaps not so many maimed bodies would have been left in the wake. For many in that movement, holiness has certainly been a simple matter to define. Don't go to movies; women, don't cut your hair or wear short-sleeved dresses or make-up; men don't use tobacco; and don't go to the store on Sunday. To be sure, many of these legalistic views of holiness are shared in full by great elements of the Pentecostal fellowship, especially the "old-liners."

Now these may *all* be admirable stands for the children of God. It is not even a point worth arguing. The real problem arises, however, when a sweet little granny who has attended three holiness camp meetings a year for 60 years tells herself she is holy because she wears no lipstick. Yet when a lovely teenage girl wearing lipstick sits near her in church, she *hates* that girl for having the audacity to be young and pretty and happy! This inconsistency between internal reality and outward appearance is, however, stuccoed tidily each year at camp meeting until it is no longer noticed. So she lives hurt, frustrated, angry, unloving and (she thinks) unloved; but she is an outward model of "holiness." With all the joy of life in a straitjacket, obeying somebody else's rules, she annually grows more insulated from the God of love.

When the face of holiness is soured by life, it is because its theology is pickled in law. John Wesley said, "Sour godliness is the devil's religion." A tragic flaw of the holiness movement has been its inability to speak meaningfully to the modern suburbanite living in a madhouse of sin. The holiness movement will continue to fail evangelistically until it broadens its vocabulary to include a few more words than "no" and "don't." Without a major revival, the holiness movement is in danger of studying Wesleyan theology while Rome burns around its ears.

Sensing intuitively that the smug Phariseeism of the holiness crowd was insufficient, many of its very children withdrew from its colleges and camp meetings to become sullen "liberals." They were not liberals by conviction but by reaction. Hence, the mainline denominations sit sulking in the corner, sucking their thumbs and whining that the "holiness hypocrites" are wrong and that the Pentecostals are stealing our members. Surely the latter is true. Those not leaving by the bus loads in broad day-light are sneaking off to see James Robison by night.

Yet neither the holiness movement nor the sulky brats in the dwindling mainline churches seem to be able to make a meaningful response.

To the legalistic and joyless holiness of one generation, the next generation may very well respond by simply throwing the baby out with the bath water.

To the paste-board "churchianity" and ersatz religion of denominations in decline, the response has often been one of incautious disregard for such basics as order, law, discipline and accountability. Charismatics have too often simply dismissed the moral implications of the Spirit-filled life. Charismatic expression in worship, the rediscovery of the gifts, the bubbling joy of the movement and its emphasis on healing are exciting to a church in serious need. The charismatic renewal has failed miserably, however, to call its rank and file to cleanness of heart and life. Its failures have often been huge, public and lurid. Hence in such a spiritual vacuum much of the so-called charismatic movement has "just growed" like Topsy. Without theological underpinnings and a deep concern for holiness, the charismatics have often seen power without direction and gifts without graces. The PTL disaster and the embarrassment of Jimmy Swaggart are a sobering warning to the charismatics and Pentecostals that power in ministry *must*—absolutely must—have holiness at its heart!

Time for Holiness and Power

It is time, *high* time, for a new call to holiness and power! Gifts and graces, liberty with order, miracles and sanctified living must grow together in a revival or it becomes lopsided and ultimately useless or even demonic.

The charismatics can continue to ignore the call of the Holy Spirit for a fresh and vigorous new emphasis on holiness only at the risk of their anointing. Continued belligerent, unscriptural attitudes among the "holiness spokesmen" toward the miracles and gifts of the Spirit will only accelerate the dangerous erosion of their ability to speak prophetically to the church. The mainline denominations can continue to vex the Holy Spirit by resisting both holiness and power and opting for business as usual, only at the expense of becoming great, lumbering dinosaurs incapable of little more than an occasional, pathetic death rattle.

I remember laughing in spite of myself at a comedian-impressionist being questioned on T.V. The comedian was brilliant. His hilarious answers were given through impressions of celebrities. I marveled that he could change from Pearl Bailey to Richard Nixon to John Wayne with such speed and facility. One exchange however deeply touched my heart.

"Don't you ever get afraid," the interviewer asked, "that you will get stuck in one character or another?"

The studio audience and I obliged the newscaster with a laugh at the odd question. But when the camera zoomed in for a close-up on the face of the comedian, he was visibly moved. The question had struck home, and his countenance sobered.

"My darkest fear," he somberly said, "is that I will wake up one morning and I'll be able to do Hubert Humphrey, Bogart and Marlene Dietrich—but I won't remember how to do *me* anymore."

Humanity's Fractured Existence

I believe that to be not only his own personal fear but also the corporate nightmare of 20th-century humanity. We contemporaries endure so fractured an existence that we are in danger of simply losing track of ourselves. We are one person at the office, another with friends, another with spouse and kids, still another at church and unlike all of the others when all alone. Depending upon who we are, there may be even more of us as we relate to a lover, boss, employee, customer, step-child, doctor, priest or lawyer.

A modern person in confrontation with a holy Christ may

well cry out, like the Gadarene demoniac, "there are many of us!" Life splintered like a mirror by a hammer blow, we search desperately for wholeness in diversion, dissipation and discipline. Confronted again and again by our own images, however, we find nothing but distortion and brokenness. Each finger of the shattered mirror may give a "true" reflection in some part. The parts, held together by a "frame" of sorts may even remain contiguous. But the jagged unavoidable reality is a shattered, pitiful reflection of the wholeness longed for.

America's long, horrifying anguish in the Watergate investigations left us nowhere to hide. The Nixonian catastrophe was not some Republican fluke marring an unbroken landscape. It was the tip of an iceberg. Corruption in politics from drunken, homosexual debauchery in the U.S. Senate to bribery and graft among county sheriffs is now accepted and even expected by the voting public.

The dismal sight of an American president swearing like a drunken sailor and covering up petty burglaries made us more than ashamed. It baptized the citizenry in paranoid fatalism, leaving many cynically dubious of the closets of their elected officials, not to mention their doctors, lawyers and even clergy. The worst of it is not that they return indicted congressmen to Washington. More distressing is that we have begun to call it "normal" that such men connive with criminals and support mistresses while faithfully attending the First Baptist Church. The abiding and fearsome sadness in much of American politics is not the criminality but the acceptable level of hypocrisy. People who have settled into broken, shattered living expect little more from their leaders. That this same cynical mentality now pervades the American religious perspective is undeniable.

Evangelists and the scandals in prominent pulpits are leaving a jaded American public reeling. Neither charismatic gifts nor holiness rules are a sufficient answer. If a religious revival is to meaningfully affect society it must reinspire a hope for wholeness and integrity. In mathematics the word "integer" means a whole number. That is, it must not be a fraction. One, four and six are integers. One-half, four and three-fifths and seven-eighths are not.

The Holy Spirit Heals the Fractured

Hence a true outpouring of the Spirit of holiness is not merely an interesting historical phenomenon. Only such an awakening can hope to produce other than fractured living by unholy men. From Ephesus to Aldersgate Street, in every great move of the Holy Spirit, whole people, sanctified people, people of integrity surfaced to change history and civilization.

The great work of the Holy Spirit is not to stamp out little, gingerbread charismatics with a cookie cutter. Nor is it to pound rebellious teenage boys into shorter hair-cuts. It is to make broken lives whole. Romans 1:4 states that Jesus was raised from the dead and declared to be the Son of God with power, by the Spirit of holiness. It is by that same Spirit of holiness that God breathes his whole life into people who are raised up from the living death of schizophrenic, shattered sin. The first time the Holy Spirit is mentioned in Scripture is in Genesis 1:2: "Now the earth was formless and empty, darkness was over the surface of the deep, and the Spirit of God was hovering over the waters."

The Wind of God blew restlessly (*brooded* would probably be the better translation) over the face of the abyss. Impatient and unsatisfied with chaos he longed to see discipline and order. God's Spirit is striving still to bring his creative character to bear on darkness and disorder. That brooding wind of God which desired to see light and life where there was darkness and chaos, now hovers achingly over the heart full of sin. The passion of the Spirit of God is to breathe upon humanity the very character and nature of God.

In a heart forgiven by God and bathed in the blood of Jesus there may still linger dark, untamed, chaotic passions more from the abyss than from above. Such people know they are redeemed. Their names are written in the Lamb's Book of Life. Blessed assurance of salvation is theirs by faith. Yet they find disillusionment at trying to walk in holiness.

Newly sensitized to the convictions of the Holy Spirit, such Christians long to be obedient, loving, whole and holy. So year after battered year they live in fierce but frustrated determination. Anger, self-loathing, depression and cynicism results.

Some are, by temperament and constitution, more resolute than others in resisting fleshly temptations. Through will power and a genuine desire to please God and obey the rules, "the flesh with the lusts thereof" is denied. Resentments, jealousies, fears, envy, unforgiveness and the corpus of spiritual sins which remain uncrucified, strip such holiness of its pious covering and reveal it to be the "will worship" (Col. 2) that it is.

Victory or Escape?

In Greek mythology the island of the Sirens seems an obvious type of sin. Sailors knew that if they drove their boats up on the rocks they would surely die, but they simply could not resist the gravitational melody. The Sirens, like sin, preyed mercilessly on passing ships, luring them to their death with their song.

Two famous captains brought their crews and ships safely past the island of the Sirens. Odysseus, knowing the danger, poured molten wax in the ears of his men and tied their hands and feet. He then strapped himself to the mast and screamed at the top of his lungs to drown the sound of the singing.

It was a victory of escape, certainly. Odysseus and his men eluded destruction, but the picture of their passage under the lee of the island is quite different from that of another ship that made the way safely.

Jason and his men, the fabled Argonauts, also escaped death on the rocks of the Sirens. Jason, however, hired a magic lute player to travel with the Argonauts. This visionary musician had the ability to totally hypnotize his hearers. Those under his spell could not break free as long as he played. As soon as Jason's ship came near the island the crew assembled on deck and the lute player began the magic melodies. The Sirens, finding their own songs ignored, listened to the lute player. At this they turned to stone, never again to lure poor sailors to death and destruction.

A great study in contrasts, typified in Jason and Odysseus, exists in the pursuit of victory in the lives of many Christians. Some, like Odysseus, seem to be strapped to the mast, wax in their ears, screaming to drown the Siren song of sin they feel drawing them to certain death. That a victory of sorts is theirs is undeniable. And when they make the harbor, safe at last, I am certain their rejoicing is great. Yet what a pathetic picture of holiness they present along the way. The sons and daughters of God are not prisoners to passion, chained against their will to the mizzen mast of dogma, longing for the deadly embrace of the Sirens.

Raised from the dead we are liberated to hear a heavenly rhapsody. It is a dreary holiness indeed that is merely resisting sin. The joy of holiness is found in having heard a sweeter song. The sweetness of sanctified living has too often been laid aside in cold-eyed haste in order to tie each other up and batten down the hatches before we can be drawn out of the way.

It is the primary work of the Holy Ghost to so thoroughly engage the soul of a believer that the drawing power of sin is snapped. Holiness is not a burden but a joy. The sanctified saint is a dancing child, turning barefoot pirouettes on the beaches of the Red Sea and singing to the desert skies. "I will sing unto the Lord for he hath triumphed gloriously! The horse and the rider are thrown into the sea" (Exodus 15:1, KJV).

The steely determination to scream right on past the island of the Sirens is admirable, of course, and certainly to be preferred over the weak resignation and moral bankruptcy of liberalism. In these last days, however, I am persuaded that the Holy Spirit longs to sound a sweeter call, "All hands on deck to hear the lute player." I do not imply that action has nothing to do with holiness. Quite the contrary! Everything we do, say and think must be brought under the captivity of the Holy Spirit.

Action, however, is the wrong place to start. If we see God as primarily holy because he does no wrong, then we begin to hammer ourselves into his sinless image. We will end up by only bringing even more brokenness into our lives. That is a classic and tragic case of "cart-before-the-horse" theology.

I do not contend that classical holiness doctrine formally teaches this dreary teeth-clenching resistance of sin. The point is that in the absence of a dynamic, explosive, personal experience of the Holy Spirit, mere doctrine will degenerate into just such a negative approach.

When, on the other hand, I throw myself before him, broken in my brokenness, he can breathe into me the Spirit of holiness which raised Christ Jesus from the dead (Rom. 1:4). Because this Spirit of holiness *is* God's wholeness, he begins to put Humpty Dumpty back together again. He begins to breathe integrity into me. He inspires purity, power and love, while filtering out sin, weakness and fear.

"Put your hand inside your cloak," God said to Moses. (Exodus 4:6-7). When Moses drew it out it was leprous. That sight must have been a shock to Moses. One can almost hear him say, "Hey, great, Lord! What a terrific miracle. You send me into Egypt where there is a price on my head. You give me 750,000 stiff-necked Jews who hate me. And now you have given me leprosy!"

But the Lord was not finished. "Now put it back into your cloak." This time when Moses drew out his hand it was clean. God may have been trying to say many things to Moses in that experience. Surely not the least among these concerned heart holiness and the ministry before him.

Outward Action Doesn't Change the Inner Person

Ultimately what we do with our hands will be a result of the condition of our heart. We cannot with an unclean heart hope to continue in an anointed ministry of power. Neither can we, by changing our outward action, hope to change the inner man.

We do not need to choose between an emphasis on holiness and an emphasis on power in ministry. Indeed, we dare not! Holiness without power is effete cleanliness. Power without holiness is dangerous and short-lived.

We must have both! We must have empowered ministries, operating in the gifts, gurgling with Pentecostal joy that is sanctified in heart and life.

In the personal life of the individual believer it is quite the same. What we do is the direct extension of the condition of our hearts. It is impossible, for example, to get a woman sanctified by forbidding her to wear skin-tight blue jeans and heavy make-up or a man sanctified by forcing him to wear swimming trunks instead of skimpy racing suits. On the other hand if his or her heart is truly surrendered to Jesus, sooner or later (probably later than the Church expects) his or her wardrobe will change also.

Holiness folks have too often over-emphasized clothes and make-up, forgetting about the heart and its attitudes. Charismatics on the other hand are often slovenly in pursuing a lifestyle reflective of simplicity, frugality, modesty and virtue.

It is troublesome indeed to see a congregation of holiness sour pusses "praising" Jesus as lifelessly and joylessly as professional mourners in Chinese funeral processions. No less worrisome however is the pervading spirit of worldliness and outright sensuality in some charismatic services. Holiness beginning at the heart will go far to bridge whatever gaps there are between charismatic and holiness believers. A new flow of the Spirit of Jesus in both will see the release of a new unfettered liberality genuinely informed by a desire to avoid all appearance of evil.

CHAPTER III

The Finger of God

❖

The Holy Spirit and the Kingdom of God

*E*yes ablaze with hellish horror, he cowered in the doorway. Shielding his face with his arms and whining like a trapped wolf, he shrank away as the Rabbi approached. The crowd watched as the Nazarene began the work of casting the demons out of the boy. There was a clash like cavalry chargers at full tilt. The nightmare wrestling match was underway. The pitiable shrieks and guttural howls were terrible to hear. Jesus of Nazareth was contesting for the spirit, mind and body of an unnamed mute held in bondage by the forces of evil. In the end the lad was free and spoke.

It was in the context of this act of deliverance (Luke 1) that Jesus gave us perhaps the greatest of all teachings on the spirit of holiness. The setting was appropriate because the spirit of God's power is less suitable for analysis in a vacuum than for demonstration in ministry. Among the great ironies of the modern church are conferences on evangelism where no one gets saved and seminars on the Holy Spirit where no one is delivered or sanctified. The storm of controversy which raged around

Jesus wherever he walked reached hurricane force on that day. Pharisees and scribes, perfectly willing for the poor, mute wretch to go on in his demonized bondage, were outraged when Jesus set him free. Their anger was more than predictable.

The most nefarious force in religion in any generation is ecclesiastical envy. The greatest opposition to sustained revival, the cruelest foes of renewal are not bar keeps and madams. They could care less. The knife at the bosom of revival power is firmly in the grip of an envious, jealous, impotent clergy unable to minister in unctionized power and unwilling for anyone else to. The petty jealousy of preachers is a constant heartache to the laity and an embarrassment to the gospel.

Heresy alone never would have crucified Jesus. In fact, it is somewhat convenient to have a few nuts about claiming to be messiah. It makes dead, pharisaical religionists look a bit better by comparison. Jesus could have stood on the steps of the temple and announced he was the Messiah or the Queen of Sheba or any other thing and hardly have drawn the wrath of the religious leaders of his own time.

It was when his word was manifested in power that Jesus sealed his own death warrant. When his sermons on the kingdom of God found expression in a ministry of power so obviously lacking among the Pharisees, their fury was predictable and deadly.

"But some of them said, 'By Beelzebub [satanic authority], the prince of demons, he is driving out demons'" (Luke 11:15).

Jesus demolished that specious logic with one sentence: "Any kingdom divided against itself will be ruined, and a house divided against itself will fall" (v. 17). In other words Jesus demanded, "Is Satan possessing such people as this and then casting himself out?" The answer was absurdly obvious and the Pharisees fell silent. Then even as he foiled their blasphemous defamation with one rhetorical question, he devastated their pride with another:

"If I drive out demons by Beelzebub, by whom do your followers drive them out?" (v. 19). That is to say, "By one power or another, they *are* out. The lad is free! He can speak! By what power do your sons, your ilk, your kind—by what power do you and yours cast out demons?"

The inescapable answer was that they could not cast them out *at all*. The penury of their ministry was brought under terrible indictment by the power of Christ's Word. Now the hellish hornet's nest of preacher-envy was shown for what it was. It was a Pandora's box of demonic, self-centered, religiosity totally incapacitated for supernatural ministry and perfectly willing to libel anyone and everyone that claimed or ministered in power beyond their experience.

The Block to Revival

In all my years of traveling evangelism I have never seen a saloon keeper fight a crusade. In fact, in Columbia, South America, a bar owner gave us rooms in which to stay. But woe to the evangelist who incurs the wrath of clergy who are more intent on protecting ecclesiastical turf than winning the lost. Hell hath no fury quite like an envious Pharisee.

The story is told of one punctilious pastor confronting Billy Sunday with protests about his methods. "Your way of doing evangelism is all wrong. Your kind of preaching, your invitations, your music, it's all wrong!"

"I 'spect you're right," Sunday replied in his inimitable manner. "But then I like the way I'm doing it wrong better than the way you ain't doing it at all."

That was the thrust of Jesus' repartee with the Pharisees. Having gained the high ground in the exchange, however, Jesus quickly pressed his advantage to give a positively foundational teaching on kingdom living in the power of the Holy Spirit. It is a rich blend of word and deed including not only the exchange with the Pharisees but also the "Lord's Prayer," the glorious promise of Luke 11:13—a declaration of God's plan and intention of restoration, *and* the call to full devotion as well. The first 23 verses of Luke 11 are perhaps the most arresting *and* challenging single body of teaching on the Holy Spirit and the kingdom of God in the New Testament.

Having summarily dismissed the challenge of the Pharisees, Jesus boldly declares, "If I drive out demons by the *finger of God*, then the kingdom of God has come to you" (v. 20, italics mine). The Finger of God means the Holy Spirit. In fact, the Matthew account uses the phrase "the Holy Spirit." Jesus' statement reveals that he saw supernatural ministry in the power of the Spirit as a confirmatory sign of the kingdom of God. "If . . . the Finger of God . . . *then* the kingdom of God . . ."

The Holy Spirit and the Second Adam

In other words, it is impossible to understand the coming of the Holy Spirit apart from the restoration of the kingdom. Failure to see the Holy Spirit as a restoration gift simply misses the broader point that God is reconciling the world to himself and *he* was its source to begin with. This same failure has often haunted "short form" evangelism such as gospel tracts. The call to "come to Jesus," is informed with its greatest attraction when the reality is reinforced that such an invitation is actually a call to "come home to Jesus."

When Adam surrendered to pride and sin he also yielded to Satan the authority and dominion to which he had been made heir. Satan's rejoicing was surely unmixed, for he knew that legally man, not God nor an angel, must reclaim that authority. The newly man-crowned "prince of the power of the air" was not about to give it back.

Adam had slammed the door on Eden but God, in grace greater than all Adam's sin, purposed to open it again. "The seed of the woman," the Spirit prophesied, "shall bruise the serpent's head."

Now, however, sin had been injected into the race. In the face of such calamity, could God hope to raise up a "new" Adam to succeed where the first one had failed? If the first Adam had sinned in an Edenic paradise how could his seed, conceived in sin and surrounded by a universe in rebellion, ever hope to "bruise the serpent's head?" Satan was in the driver's seat and he knew it.

The one utterly incalculable act of God that spelled the end of Satan's reign was the Incarnation. That in the womb of a virgin the personal expression of God might become human flesh *and* the second Adam was one possibility that had certainly eluded the Gates of Hell.

Jesus said, "When a strong man, fully armed, guards his own house, his possessions are safe" (Luke 11:21). The "strong man" was Satan who, armed with a demonic host and cast out of heaven in rebellion, kept his house (a fallen universe) and his goods (the sons and daughters of Adam). The "someone stronger" was the Word who became flesh. Satan held each of us captive in a purse at his side until Jesus met him in the way and committed highway robbery!

When Jesus sent out the 70 for ministry he commanded them to heal the sick, cast out demons and preach the gospel.

What gospel? They could hardly have preached the blood of Jesus while it still flowed in his veins. The cross and the resurrection were yet to be accomplished. What, then, *did* they preach? God is now here in your midst! The kingdom of God has launched a beach-head in alien territory. The seed of woman has finally come! The prophetic utterances and mirrored images of the One stronger who should come were hardly more than out-croppings of a distant mountain. Closer still was John the Baptist who proclaimed the kingdom to be "at hand." To the oft repeated prophecy of a coming Messiah, John added a note of immediate urgency. His call was to a personal repentance and a state of preparedness to receive the one stronger who was to appear and rescue Adam's race from the strong man. The Baptist's life and ministry found fulfillment in his climactic announcement, "Look, the Lamb of God, who takes away the sin of the world" (John 1:29).

By his sin, the first Adam closed the door on Eden, by his righteousness, the second Adam threw it wide open again. The first Adam brought death. The second Adam brought life! The first Adam brought the curse. The second Adam bore it. The first Adam sealed humanity out. The second Adam sealed humanity in. The manifest proof that Jesus was the second Adam now back to overcome the strong man was his ministry in the power of the Finger of God.

The Finger of God

The trail of that phrase, the Finger of God, in the Old Testament is highly provocative. Rarely employed, it surfaces with impact at significant moments. The Finger of God actually means *the Holy Spirit*. Moses and Aaron sought by demonstration of power before Pharaoh to persuade Egypt to release the Hebrews. In an obvious effort to belittle the supernatural acts, Pharaoh summoned his own magicians. When Aaron's rod became a serpent, so did those of the magicians. Now certainly Aaron came out ahead in each case, but it was a "split decision." The conclusion might well have been reached that Aaron and the Egyptian magicians were both dealing in the profane powers of ancient witchcraft, albeit with Aaron being slightly the more proficient. This was put to lie, however, when Aaron called forth lice out of the dust. *This* the Egyptian wizards could not even begin to imitate (Ex. 7:10-11; 8:16-18).

"Your majesty," they were saying in their frustration, "this is the *Finger of God*." That is to say, "We are not just being outdone in the power of evil. Moses and Aaron are not simply better wizards than we. They represent another kingdom beyond Egypt, beyond wizardry. *This* is the *Finger* of *God*."

"The magicians said to Pharaoh, 'This is the Finger of God.' But Pharaoh's heart was hard and he would not listen, just as the Lord had said" (Ex. 8:19).

In Exodus 9 the phrase implies power. By this miraculous

power Moses performed the works that delivered Israel from
Egypt. In Luke 11, Jesus himself said that it was by the Finger
of God that he delivered the boy from demons.

The phrase *Finger of God* reappears dramatically in Exodus
31:18. Here the law is written by the Finger of God. Very similar to Zechariah 14:20, it is the Finger of God which inscribes
the law of separation and holiness.

The contrast is clear and startling from the New Testament
perspective. We Christians love to point out that we are no longer
bound by the law. Yet it is the Finger of God which writes the
law, and it is by the Finger of God that Jesus works the works
of deliverance.

Can the Finger of God write both liberty *and* law? Is the
Holy Spirit the Finger of God which sanctifies men and women
or is he the Finger of God which empowers them for miracles
to turn the Nile to blood and cast out demons?

Now the contrasting insights on the Holy Spirit afforded by
these passages is substantially the tension between the charismatic and holiness schools.

In his prophecy of the coming covenant Jeremiah shines the
needed light. "'This is the covenant I will make with the house
of Israel after that time,' declares the Lord. 'I will put my law in
their minds and write it on their hearts. I will be their God, and
they will be my people'" (Jeremiah 31:33).

This passage from Jeremiah is crucial to any understanding
of the Holy Spirit's work. It was this insight that the Pharisees
missed. They hoped to make themselves holy by obeying the
law. Too often the holiness movement has missed as well. These
people have frequently hoped an inward change would finally
follow sufficient outward observance. Tragically, the charismatics have usually missed it as well. Laying aside the "tithe of mint
and cumin" they have, all too often, lost all hope of *any* kind of
change, outward *or* inward!

Because God is eternal so is his Word. In Leviticus 19:2, the
God of Moses said, "Be holy because I [I AM], the Lord your
God, am holy." He did not mean, "this is in effect until the com-

ing of Messiah." I AM is holy yesterday, today and forever. Because "I AM is holy, my people shall be holy," yesterday, today and forever.

The Finger of God and Holiness

The great and glorious good news, however, is that holiness in the new kingdom shall be in the image of the holiness of I AM. Jeremiah prophesied that it should be a matter of the heart not outward observance. Hence the disciples of Christ must exceed the Pharisees in holiness, not by obeying the law better than they—they were, after all, quite good at it—but by demonstrating the spirit of the law.

When John proclaimed Jesus of Nazareth the "Lamb of God" he also said that Jesus was "he who will baptize with the Holy Spirit." (John 1:33). In other words, John viewed the coming of the kingdom to signal the dawn of a new era. He saw that in the kingdom of the Messiah the baptism of the Holy Spirit would be a reality.

The gospel the 70 preached, the weight of John's message and the reality that the demons feared was the restoration of the kingdom. He, with authority to minister by the Finger of God, had come to reclaim his own. Remember, John said he would know the Messiah by virtue of the Holy Spirit resting upon him. The *shekinah* glory had rested above the mercy seat in the tabernacle. Now the Word had condescended to share the tabernacle with men. The tabernacle in the wilderness was drab and plain on the outside but beautiful on the inside and full of glory. Jesus may have been as the prophet Isaiah said "not comely that we should desire him." But the Holy Spirit rested on him in power like the *shekinah* glory. The devils knew and trembled. John saw and rejoiced. The Pharisees beheld and blasphemed. But they all sensed the truth. Immanuel had come.

It is impossible to understand the Holy Spirit or his work in the life of the believer. In fact, it is impossible to really understand the work of Calvary or full redemption or the kingdom of God or the gospel by starting with the lostness of humanity. It is essential to biblical truth that we start with paradise lost. The essence is not that sinful humanity can be forgiven; it is far, far more. It is that a squandered kingdom is being restored.

The problem was not that the Pharisees did not observe the law outwardly. They did on the whole. It was rather that they were white-washed tombs, as Jesus said. They gleamed white and shining in sun but were full of dead men's bones on the inside.

The heart of holiness in the kingdom is to *be* the heart. Jeremiah 31 says the law will still be written in the kingdom when Messiah comes. It will, however, no longer be written in tablets of stone. The New Covenant will see the law written in the innermost part, the heart of mankind.

Hence, the law of holiness has not been set aside. We are, however, called into a relational change with the law. If we opt for a mere legalism, the stone tablets of the law become our prison house. This is where many in the classical holiness denominations stand. Shoulder to the wheel, nose to the grindstone they cry, "Today I shall be holy if it kills me!" It will! It surely will. That makes the good news bad news.

Yet if we simply cast aside the law of holiness in the name of grace, we disregard the very claim of God and the whole council of Scripture. Holiness is no New Testament superfluity. In Romans 6:1-4, Paul speaks to this very idea.

What shall we say then? Shall we go on sinning so that grace may increase? By no means! We died to sin, how can we live it any longer? Or don't you know that all of us who were baptized into Jesus Christ were baptized into his death? We were therefore buried with him through baptism into death in order that, just as Christ was raised from the dead through the glory of the Father, we too may live a new life. (KJV).

The casual disregard among many charismatics for the biblical call to such *newness of life* must be stopped. Otherwise

we shall continue to have so-called leaders in the charismatic
movement deserting the brides of their youth and living lives of
conspicuous consumption on the contributions of the sincere.

Without some serious thought and heartfelt repentance, we
are in danger of developing, in the name of grace and the blessings of the kingdom, a moral posture somewhere to the left of
whoopee. Shall our liberty now become license? God forbid!

In a small town in Northern Georgia I found a small church
named the Bypass Holiness Church. I have known many
churches that were trying to bypass holiness. I just never saw it
advertised before. In a juvenile over-reaction to legalistic holiness, shall we burn down the house just to clean the carpets? The
church cannot bypass holiness.

In every generation the Finger of God does exactly what he
did on Sinai's craggy brow; he writes the law of holiness. It is
our relationship to that law which determines the shape of our
lives. *Under* the law we become bound and brittle. *Outside* the
law we become rebellious, proud and sinful. In Jeremiah 31:33,
however, we see that there remains still a third possibility. No
longer *under* the law that it might constrain us and never *outside* the law that it might condemn us. But the law is *within* us
that it might convert us.

The great work of the Holy Spirit is still to write the law.
Now in the kingdom he will no longer carve it in stone to stand
in implacable, impersonal judgment on all men. He writes instead in the inner sanctum of the soul, HOLY TO THE LORD.
Hence the law becomes a living fountain of grace in man's inner
being, rather than a straight and narrow inlet only for those of
resolute will.

A Balance of Holiness and Power

By seeing the Holy Spirit as the Finger of God, the apparent
tension between the emphases of holiness and power is fully
met. He is both. It is the Finger of God who writes the law of

God but it is also by, and in, the Finger of God that the Church's hope of a supernatural ministry is fulfilled. The Holy Spirit rested on Jesus to utterly sanctify his life, and by it he cast out demons, healed the sick and raised the dead.

The idiotic cloud of suspicion that hangs in the air whenever holiness and charismatic (or Pentecostal) Christians discuss the work of the Holy Spirit must be dispelled. The Finger of God writes the law of holiness in the heart of the believer. This great work of heart holiness cannot be over-estimated. To lose sight of it is to lose all. However, it must also be remembered that it is by the power of this same Finger of God that Jesus wrought miracles, discerned spirits and cast out devils. A balanced hope of sanctification and a ministry of charismatic power is a holy wedlock indeed. It is a marriage made in heaven, a mirror of Christ, the heartbeat of New Testament Christianity.

Now the question remains, "Can I, in my humanity, receive the Spirit of holiness that rested on Jesus?" Is this a "kingdom principle" more to be debated than realized? Or is this a personal possibility? Why certainly John saw the Holy Spirit rest on Jesus Christ. He was, after all, exactly that, the Christ of God. It is impossible, however, to imagine a believer not painfully aware of his or her humanity.

Often in a deep consciousness of Christ's divinity it is easy to lose sight of his humanity. Hence it is often forgotten that this two-fold work of sanctification and empowerment done in Jesus by the Holy Spirit epitomizes that which he longs to do in *all* believers. John the Baptist said that he on whom the Holy Spirit rested would also be him who bestowed it. Certainly Jesus had no need of being cleansed from sin. Yet the point remains that the Holy Spirit came, filling and glorifying a human vessel. Holiness and power resided fully in Christ.

The Lord himself devoted considerable time in the passage to a clarion emphasis on the willingness of God to pour his Spirit into patently human "seekers." In a series of rather obvious parables (the midnight visitor, the hungry child, the bread, the fish and the egg) Jesus is clearly hoping to demonstrate the willingness of God to baptize humanity in the Holy Spirit.

"If you then, though you are evil, know how to give good gifts to your children, how much more will your Father in heaven give the Holy Spirit to those who ask him!" (Luke 11:13).

What God Did With His Son

Many years ago a medical missionary in West Africa was visited by an inquisitive bishop. The bishop toured the hospital, met the patients, saw the many churches which had been built and sensed the general spirit of revival. "Tell me," the bishop said, "about your first convert here. How long were you here before your first conversion?"

"Four years, bishop," he replied. "When we first came to this country, the people utterly rejected my gospel. They would not even hear it. They came to the clinic. They accepted my medicine. But no matter what I did they wouldn't even come in the chapel I built or listen to me in the open. But our first child was born shortly after we arrived. He was a sweet little fellow that I loved more than life itself. When he was four years old he contracted a jungle fever and died. It hit me like a hammer blow. I dug his little grave in a clearing and buried him with my own hands. Then I fell on my knees and sobbed. Four years of frustration, hurt and disillusionment flowed out of me in a river of tears. I looked up and saw the village chief watching me. I had been declaring the victory of Christ for four years, now here I was blubbering like a baby at our first real crisis. That only made me weep more!

"Suddenly the chief ran screaming into the village where he assembled all the people and told me that they would hear my message. I stood up and preached by my son's little grave and many were saved that day."

"What was he yelling to the others?" the astonished bishop asked.

"He weeps!" answered the doctor.

"The chief also shouted, 'Come quickly, the missionary is a real man. Come let us go out to hear him.'

"You see, bishop," the missionary continued, "I arrived here with my white skin and pale eyes, and they thought I wasn't altogether human. But in death and pain they saw my humanity unmasked and they came into the kingdom."

"But wait," the flustered bishop exclaimed. "That is against everything I believe about the goodness of God. Are you telling me that your little son had to die that they could come into the kingdom?"

"I am only a doctor," the missionary replied. "You are the theologian. But it seems to me that is what God did with his Son."

That is *exactly* what God did! "Although he was a son, he learned obedience from what he suffered" (Hebrews 5:8). In the agony of the cross Christ proved forever the reality of his humanity. In his life and ministry he proved the power of the Holy Spirit within him, the Spirit of holiness in an earthen vessel. "Ask," he said, "and you shall receive."

We must vigilantly disallow any aspersions on God's willingness to baptize believers with the Holy Spirit. Jesus said "to them that ask." Why then are we not filled? Since God is not the variable, the answer must lie either in the seeker or in the seeking or both.

The true Pentecostal blessing will not be found by glib experience-mongers hoping for a slightly higher-volt tingle. Baptism in the Spirit is the fruit of full surrender, not the coincidental fall-out from being "slain in the Spirit." It is no accident that both the record of Christ's ministry of deliverance in Luke 11 and his teaching on the Holy Spirit are prefaced by the Lord's Prayer. In the day of the promise of Luke 11:13, the condition of verse two is easily overlooked. "Thy kingdom come. Thy will be done, as in heaven, so in earth" (KJV).

The Master proved that he was the master teacher by the progression he developed in Luke 11:1-23.

The will of God . . . The kingdom of God . . . The Spirit of

God . . . The Finger of God . . .

There is no small body of literature being poured out today on the kingdom of God. This is usually with particular emphasis on the rights, privileges, priorities and blessings of its citizenry. Gratuitous references to prosperity and general blessedness have reached the saturation point in much contemporary Christian writing and music. And certainly the blessedness of the children of the King is not even arguable. Who would *want* to argue it? However that is the funny thing about kingdoms. A kingdom is not a kingdom without a king.

In the mad dash to the blessing table the church must remember exactly who is Lord there. The key which unlocks the power of the kingdom is the kingship of Christ. Jesus said it as simply as possible.

"Thy kingdom come. Thy will be done in earth, as it is in heaven" (Matt. 6:10, KJV). Whenever our will is done we live in our kingdom. When his will is done we live in his. The prayer that gains the full blessing of Pentecost is the prayer of full surrender to the lordship of Jesus Christ. We do not have to "talk God out of" the baptism. He is, after all, not an ungracious host reluctant to leave his snug bed to serve bread to a short-sighted neighbor with unexpected house-guests. He longs and aches to pour his Holy Spirit into ready vessels. He absolutely will *not* however, fill a vessel which he does not own.

When we declare our Savior to be our King we begin to live in his kingdom. We can, by asking in faith, be baptized in the Spirit of his own holiness. He comes in wind and fire to cleanse us *and* to empower us as his agents, invested with full power to transact his business.

This blessed Holy Spirit, the Finger of God that he is, writes the law of holiness in our hearts even as he throws open the way into the ministry of supernatural New Testament, healing, soul-winning, miracle power!

I have already said it is not necessary that we choose between an emphasis on personal holiness and an empowered, gifted ministry. In fact, we *dare* to do so at our own peril. The

Finger of God is the Spirit of holiness, the vehicle of sanctifying grace. At the same time, it is only by his power that this poor demonized, wounded, sin-sick world has any hope of healing power in the Church.

Some have sought the gifts of the Spirit and failed wretchedly to bear his fruit. Still others have shot miserably wide of the mark, in a well-meaning over-correction, by rejecting the gifts in which Jesus himself ministered. The tragedy of forgotten holiness is heart-rending. The pathetic powerlessness of a giftless, "right-thinking" ministry is equally sad in the light of desperation of the hour.

Come Holy Spirit.

Blow breath of God, we pray. In loving restlessness come brood across the face of Christ's Church; convict us of sin and powerlessness.

Break us, O Lord, until we really face our need of you, and cry out a prayer of soul surrender.

Then write, blessed Finger of God, the law of holiness within and pour your gifts out through us that the world might see and know that the God of miracles lives.

In Jesus' Name.

CHAPTER IV

Power, Not power

❖

Power in the Kingdom and the World

Acts 1:8: "Lord, are you at this time going to restore the kingdom to Israel?" one of the apostles asked.

Expectant faces turned to Jesus. Hope flickered in their eager eyes. Jesus knew what they were thinking. They were still waiting for him to topple the Roman empire and set up his throne (and theirs) in Jerusalem. John the Baptist had said the ax was at the root.

Jesus' answer was only another confusing piece in the already confusing jigsaw puzzle of their lives with him. The apostles had struggled to comprehend the events in which they lived for three years. They saw Jesus' miracles, his healing grace, even his power to raise the dead, and they wondered. "Who is this?" They asked themselves, "Could he actually be the coming king?" He did not really act like a king.

Gradually the unthinkable intruded upon their thinking. Their imaginations began to entertain the unimaginable. Finally Peter articulated the startling conclusion, "You are the Christ, the Son of the living God!" This astonishing revelation meant

they were, in their own generation, actually seeing the hope of
Israel come to pass. How thrilling that great moment as they paraded into Jerusalem in his shadow to the cheers of the people.
The shouts of the people rang in their ears.

"Hosanna to the King!"

First-century Israel, especially religious leaders, expected
Messiah to be some kind of iron-age Moshe Dayan. They had
envisioned Messiah rolling into Jerusalem standing in the turret
of a Sherman tank, turning his guns on the Romans and blasting the Atonia Fortress to pieces. Many harbored a gleeful hope
of seeing Roman centurions nailed to their own crosses. Yes, the
coming of Messiah would surely re-establish the Davidic dynasty and shatter the hateful yoke of gentile oppression.

That Jesus failed to do so was manifestly obvious. His own
crucifixion finished off that hope. Yet now his resurrection has
breathed fresh life into the dream. Perhaps, reasoned the apostles, perhaps *now* he could crush Rome and claim his throne.

What Kind of Power?

The word "power" was and remains a key problem for the
church. What did Jesus mean by *power*? Jesus had that unique
way of using words to communicate at two simultaneous levels.
Now Jesus seemed to dismiss as simply beyond their concern
the power of an earthly principality in Jerusalem. At the same
time he promised them "power when the Holy Spirit comes upon
you."

It appeared that Jesus was saying, "Forget about power. That
is not your concern. Instead, receive Power. Receive *Power* not
power." What could he mean?

They wanted a warrior prince in whose kingdom they would
also share power. The priestly clan chafed under the rule of the
Romans. When Messiah came he would surely restore them to
rightful power and put these gentile dogs in their place. Jesus,
far from giving any encouraging signs toward that end, seemed

to threaten whatever little shreds of power they *had* managed to keep.

It was true! Now they knew it was true. Jesus was the King, and it is the business of kings to set up kingdoms. It was so like this eccentric Nazarene to enter Jerusalem riding on the colt of an ass. Yet they had no doubt that he had entered to claim his kingdom. The shouts of the people heralded the kingdom's beginning.

Then just on the brink of his momentous victory, the kingdom was snatched from his (and their) hands. Arrested, tortured and crucified by Jewish and gentile leaders who feared him, Jesus' meteoric rise to power was stopped dead in one night.

Their kingdom hopes were entombed with him. A dead messiah is no messiah at all, and a kingdom that might have been is just one more thwarted pipe dream.

Then suddenly on the third day an hysterical woman, an ex-prostitute to boot, claimed to have seen him alive. The tomb was indeed empty, but what did it mean? Others claimed a visitation on the road to Emmaus.

Finally Thomas put into words what the rest had feared to say. "But he said to them, 'Unless I see the nail marks in his hands and put my finger where the nails were, and put my hand into his side, I will not believe it'" (John 20:25).

In other words, Thomas said, "I cannot face another disappointment." Who could blame him? Had anyone's emotions ever undergone such a horrifying itineration as had the apostles? The kingdom expected, doubted, then believed, then claimed, then lost. This resurrected hope of the kingdom needed some fleshed-out reality for Thomas.

Suddenly that very reality appeared before them. Jesus walked through the wall of the room as he had penetrated the walls of the tomb. Resurrection had conquered death!

This was the final manifest proof of the *kingdom*. Jesus' words about the "kingdom of God" were not just rhetoric after all. In that astonishing, breathing moment they must surely have sensed something of the reality of the Master's cryptic words to the Pharisees. They remembered how Jesus had spoken of his own ministry of deliverance (Luke 11) as the Finger of God. He had stated in no uncertain terms that such "Finger of God" power was proof that the kingdom had "come upon" them.

"No one can enter a strong man's house and carry off his possessions unless he first ties up the strong man. Then he can rob his house" (Mark 3:27). The "strong man" they understood to be Satan, therefore surely mankind itself was the "possessions." Satan kept man in his kingdom's bondage—cycle of sin and death—by the legal authority of Adam's rebellion. Satan's only fear was that the great King, the seed of the woman, would somehow return to claim his own.

God had now proven Jesus to be the rightful heir, the scion of the kingdom of God, by his resurrection from the dead. Jesus as the first born from the dead now stood before them, and their weak faith reclaimed what the crucifixion had stolen from them—the hope of the kingdom of God in Jesus Christ.

Now one great question remained. What would the kingdom's advent mean in *their lives?* Jesus was alive for sure. With him, their hopes of the kingdom were resurrected. Yet they continued to wonder about the expression of kingdom.

Corrupting Power

The power of this world stands in stark contrast with the Power of the kingdom of God. Such power derives from the rebellion of Satan. They always ultimately rest their authority in the security of force. The world's power finds expression in avarice, sensuality, corruption, manipulation and brutality. The entire world system and idealogies, political, economical and relational, are quite simply variations on one theme: *domination is power.*

The kingdom of God is based solely on the ultimate authority of the one true King. He who is I AM will judge all ideologies, world systems, structures and nations. He transcends them all. Therefore those who live and move in him are in and of his kingdom. His kingdom finds expression in holiness, love and truth. The key to Power in the kingdom of God is not domination but submission to the King.

Hence every structure, system, ideology and individual falls into one of these two. Either we are of the kingdom of God, or we are of the rebellion. We seek either the manifestation of *his* power to *his* glory or we seek power for ourselves to our glory. These kingdoms are locked in combat in every realm, spiritual and physical.

Upon consideration of the historical perspective, the enmity, malevolence and subtlety of the rebellion is obvious. Since Lucifer was hurled from heaven, he and his demons have propagated the rebellion by brutality and cunning. They have used kings and bishops alike. They have inspired the murder of prophets, corrupted men of faith, despoiled the innocent, made mockery of the holy, persecuted the pure, made preachers into politicians and turned popes into pirates. The rebellion is *always* against God and his authority.

Satan's ability to spiritually inform both sides of worldly conflicts is bitter indeed. The Latin American dictator who uses torture and intimidation to maintain control is of the rebellion. Ironically so is the liberation theologian who makes a mockery of the Scripture, justifies murderous methods and mouths Marxist mantras to gain power. Both are rebellious to God. His kingdom will stand in judgement on them both.

The church itself is the bitterest battleground because it is the entity on earth closest to the King. The rebellion seeks to brutally crush the true church when it can. When it cannot, it will instead grant gold and worldly power. In other words if Satan cannot brutalize the church he will corrupt it, and nothing corrupts quite like power.

In the entire history of the church God has raised up voices of renewal calling for the restoration of the kingdom's Power and holiness. The voices of revival have always been opposed, at least as vehemently, by those in ecclesiastical power as by the secular world.

The Power of the Holy Spirit is the manifestation of the kingdom. Where God's kingship is honored the Finger of God will move in healing power. By the same token, where the agenda of the world is adopted by the church and pursued by worldly means, the Satanic kingdom of antichrist is furthered.

Religious power Fighting God's Power

Herod killed John the Baptist. Caiaphas conspired to murder Jesus. The Pope excommunicated Martin Luther. Wesley was banned from Anglican pulpits. The Methodists dismissed William Booth. The *real* issue in the ecclesiastical opposition to revival is seldom theological. The issue is: Who's in charge here? Power is the crux of the problem.

Whenever bishops jealously guard their own little kingdoms against the resurgent Power of God's kingdom they stand, like the Pharisees in Luke 11, in contradiction to the Finger of God. The Pharisees accused Jesus of manipulation and demagoguery. In fact they even went so far as to label as demonic his ministry of deliverance.

Jesus made it perfectly clear that in so doing they were part of the rebellion, *not* of the kingdom. "He who is not with me is against me." In other words, how can one be in the kingdom of God and fight the flow of kingdom power for the sake of the preservation of some dead religious structure?

The substitution of power politics for Pentecostal Power is not just an impediment to revival, it is the essence of satanic revival. It is the kingdom against *the* Kingdom, power against Power, the very spirit of antichrist.

This has little to do with one's theological persuasion. The "charismatic" layman who uses gossip and conspiracy to dislodge a "non-charismatic" pastor is himself actually playing into the hands of the rebellion. For the furtherance of the Power of the kingdom of God one may not employ the power of the kingdom of antichrist. One of Satan's favorite ploys is to entice folks who are right-thinking theologically to use satanic means for the sake of the kingdom.

The problem is, of course, that the powerless are less tempted to oppose the Power of God. That is the reason the Scriptures say "the common people heard him gladly." They had no religious office to guard against the kingdom. Those in power must constantly check their spirits for signs of the rebellion.

The college president is more likely to oppose a genuine move of God on campus than would a first-quarter freshman. The bishop will guard the status quo more carefully than the pastor of a five-point circuit in South Alabama simply because the status quo suits him better. If a local church begins to experience the free flow of revival Power, the district superintendent may be tempted to move the pastor and replace him with a "company man," not on theological grounds but because revivals make those in power suspicious.

A move of the Spirit always produces a manifestation of King Jesus. The kingdom of darkness always tries to abort such fruit. Pharaoh and Herod committed genocide to stop the kingdom. Caiaphas killed the Messiah to guard his own little petty throne. The bishop and cabinet which move a charismatic pastor to stop what is happening in his church aborts the kingdom before the manifestation of Power can in anyway inhibit their own power.

The Power of the Finger of God in ministry is the kingdom of God in action. The power of the world in political machinations and petty manipulative little schemes is the king of darkness in action. They are opposed, the one to the other, even as God and Lucifer are.

God's Power Comes to the Weak

God longs to manifest his Power in our lives and ministries but he cannot as long as we are content to seek our own power.

We may have Power or power but we may not have both.
Here is the crux of the matter:
"My will be done. My kingdom come," or
"Thy will be done. *Thy* kingdom come."
The kingdom of God will never come by power. And Power
will never come by the kingdom of this world. We cannot secure the kingdom by force of rebellion. That is "liberation theology," and it is satanic. We cannot buy the kingdom. Simon the
Magician attempted to do that in Acts 8, and Peter the Apostle
discerned the satanic influence at work. "Thou hast neither part
nor lot in this matter . . . For I perceive that thou art in the gall
of bitterness, and in the bond of iniquity" (Acts 8: 21, 23, KJV).

What did Peter mean by "this matter"? Obviously he meant
the manifestation of genuine kingdom ministry. *That* cannot be
bought. We may simulate it with Hollywood glamour and tele-
vision glitz but we cannot generate the Power and we cannot
purchase it. The kingdom is not up for grabs to the revolution-
aries who overthrow the "tyranny of Rome." Neither is it for sale
to the highest bidder.

In Acts 1, the apostles hoped Jesus would throw off the yoke
of Roman oppression, and he spoke of *Power* instead. In Acts
8, Simon Magus tried to buy an anointed ministry and Peter said
"Thy money perish with thee."

It is an ironic twist of church history that radical liberation-
ists, power-hungry district superintendents and glitzy T.V.
preachers may actually spring from the same source. The kingdom is not for gun-toting nuns, nor to glib power-brokers trading votes to get elected bishop nor yet to the mink-draped
miniatures of super-star religion.

Years ago I traveled to Mexico with my old friend Jim Mann,
a Pentecostal lay-missionary. I had invited several American pastors to accompany us in hopes of interesting them in Jim's precious work. We stopped in McAllen, Texas, to buy the insurance
for driving in Mexico and to gas up the van. As we preachers
waited in the van, Jim got out to talk to the young black station
attendant.

"Tonight we will have a service near Victoria." I said. "I'd like for one of you guys to preach."

That immediately launched them into a strident argument about whom it should be. I instantly regretted not having just chosen one. Their petty bickering and the Texas heat drove me out of the van in search of Jim and the attendant who were no longer in sight.

I discovered them in the station's squalid "office" kneeling on the bare floor. I listened with tears in my eyes as they prayed together the sinner's prayer. The irony of it was obvious. In the van sat Methodist pastors who for all their education and ordination managed only a futile squabble, while a bald-headed old contractor with a "Jacob's limp" led a soul to Christ.

In the weak God will manifest his strength. To the poor in spirit, the kingdom will come in Power. To the "ignorant and unlearned" who yield all to God's authority, the kingdom will come in *POWER*.

CHAPTER V

The Man in the Monkey Suit

❖

THE INNER WORK AND THE OUTER IMAGE

Desperate for employment, a depression-era farmer applied at a passing circus. At the circus office door he made an impassioned plea.

"I'll do anything," he begged.

At this the manager's eyes lit up. "You're hired," he fairly shouted, embracing the shocked indigent. "I need a new gorilla. The old one has died, and we cannot afford to import one. We have skinned old Kong out, and I need someone to wear the suit and do the gorilla act."

All reluctance dissolved at the mention of a sizable salary. Pride gave way to necessity and the farmer's new career was launched. As it turned out the wheat farmer turned ape-man rather enjoyed it. His act was dramatic and crowd pleasing. He would swing out over the lion's cage on a rope and chatter excitedly at the enraged beast below. The rope was carefully measured, however, and any actual danger seemed minimal.

In a kiddie matinee in Oklahoma a miscalculation brought catastrophe, and he tumbled into the lion's cage. The lion leapt upon him immediately, and placing a massive paw on either of the "gorilla's" shoulders, began to roar in his face.

"Help," screamed the man in the gorilla costume. "Help me! Someone please save me."

"Shut up, you fool!" the lion whispered in his ear. "You'll get us *both* fired."

Unhappily a great deal of what passes for true Christianity is nothing more than monkey-suit religion. The calamitous condition of the contemporary church is that she has a pretty fair idea of what a Christian looks like. Hence she can, if only for short periods of time and with varying degrees of success, imitate it. Granted, the view may be informed by local or cultural differences and some may be more gifted than others at articulating it, but the fact remains that an immutable portrait of a "Christian" has achieved something of a universal, if somewhat shadowy, consensus. The primitive church at, say Colossae, in the first century A.D. had no such luxury. "Christian" had never existed before, and the pedantic definitions of "churchmanship" awaited the arrival of the 20th century.

As Paul preached revival power exploded in the streets of a Turkish seaport named Ephesus. The flames of burning magic books lit the blue-collar neighborhoods near the waterfront. There was an initial outpouring of the Holy Ghost, accompanied by a variety of spiritual gifts which gave rise to a general spirit of conviction. The longing for holiness among Ephesus' new converts began almost immediately to cut into the profits of the local purveyors of idolatry. Revival quickly turned to riot, and Paul reluctantly yielded to the pleas of his friends and moved to higher ground. He did not leave, however, before the seeds of revival were airborne. Carried by the wind the gospel swept upstream from the low rent districts of Ephesus to the penthouse luxury of Laodicea and hot springs of Colossae.

There the church bloomed wild. Without benefit of proper clergy or church growth experts, the churches of Colossae and

Laodicea sprang to life in the white heat of revival. Later as wolves came upon them with the impossible burdens of law, that precious innocence of early faith began to corrode. The despair of perfectionism is the poisonous byproduct when revival power is besotted by legal holiness.

In Colossians 1:27, Paul moved past even the basic problem of the law versus grace for salvation. In that brilliant passage he dealt with an even more fundamental issue. How do I live as a Christian? What does it even mean to live a holy life? What is the secret of true holiness?

"The secret," Paul said, "is Christ in you, the hope of glory."

The Non-Option of Pentecost

On the surface it may not appear much of a secret. The implications however are magnificent. The secret of the gospel and of holiness which was hidden from Moses and Abraham is now revealed in the Church. That secret is not some new way to attain the strength necessary to obey the law. It is not some heretofore hidden pathway of meditation and mystical experience now revealed only to a monastical elite. The secret is simply the indwelling fullness of Christ in the earthen vessels of human beings.

Of course Paul was writing in Greek, but the Hebrew word for "glory" pertains. That word (*kabod*) has a variety of meanings. All of them seem to give new insight. The first is the idea of weight, as when a king's signet ring is pressed into wax. The pressure or weight of the ring leaves behind the imprint of the glory of the ring. There is, I suppose, a sense in which we may say that we, like Jesus, bear the stamped image of the Father (Col. 1).

The deeper, more precious meaning has more to do with atmosphere than with mass. It implies an alteration in ambience due to the presence of a high official. It speaks of that sudden, magical charge in the air at the arrival of some person of note.

I was asked to pray before the inauguration of Georgia's Governor, Joe Frank Harris. As a result my wife and I were also invited to attend the Inaugural Ball. Hundreds of couples jammed the ballroom, dancing half-heartedly to some tired-sounding band. The elderly men for all the world resembling polish sausages in their too-tight cummerbunds and the over made-up women who had been crammed into their girdles for hours seemed more than a little lifeless to my wife and me. We were excited at being at our first inauguration and thrilled at seeing a Christian elected to such high office, but the whole sad, sagging evening was a lackluster disappointment indeed.

Suddenly without any announcement the room came alive! The band sat up straight, the torture of high heels and tuxedos was forgotten, and every eye strained for a view of the one person who made sense of the whole absurd evening. The room was electrified because the governor had arrived! The glory (*kabod*) of his office was having its immediate effect on the very atmosphere. A Christian's life should experience a detectable change at the presence of a high official. When the King of Kings and the Lord of Lords dwells in the throne room of any heart, that life will give manifest testimony to his residence. The life so indwelt will have about it a *glo*-ry, a radiance, an aura (if that word has not been debased beyond use by spiritualists).

It is this very inner change, effecting an outer witness to which the saints of God from Simon Peter to H. C. Morrison have testified. Some have called it the second blessing or the second work of grace or the deeper work or the higher path or the fullness of Pentecost. John the Baptist called it being baptized with fire and with the Holy Ghost (Luke 3:16). Jesus used the same terminology in Acts 1. Call it the baptism with the Holy Spirit or call it the second touch. It does not matter so much what you call it. It matters very much that you have it.

The filling of the Holy Spirit is *not* optional. It is not for those who are somehow into that sort of thing. It is God's command that we receive it and his promise that we may.

The heart baptized in the Holy Spirit becomes a spring of

living water. As the inner heart of a person is changed, his or her outward life will necessarily change. Holiness hence becomes less a matter of obeying rules and more a matter of partaking of the divine nature (2 Peter 1:4).

Limitation of the Monkey Suit

What a glorious promise! I will act differently because I *am* different. Attitudes, desires, hopes, longings and aspirations will finally reveal who is in charge within. As Stephen fell, bloodied and broken, beneath the stones of hatred and prejudices, he spoke the words of Jesus and had the countenance of an angel. The *real* Stephen, stripped of all facade, was clearly revealed in pain, humiliation and death. Stephen showed what he was made of in that moment (Acts 7:60).

He was a man full of faith and the Holy Spirit (v. 55).

The unctionless American pulpit is a modern tragedy. Even sadder is the host of nice, decent, saved, church-going housewives who find themselves weeping into the dishwasher every morning when the kids leave for school with no idea why. They know something is missing and do not know what to ask for.

It is for their sakes and for businessmen, high school students, missionaries and believers of every age and station who cannot seem to find the flow of real life in their faith that the baptism with the Holy Spirit must be preached. They have believed for salvation and often can articulate their assurance well, but they are unable to love, live, give and forgive in any liberty. They probably are even aware of the Holy Spirit as a comforter, guide and companion. They have *not* however found that great release of the Spirit whereby he flows out from them in a river of life.

Because their good, conservative, Bible-belt understanding of what a Christian looks like is pretty clearly defined, they are able, over the years, to hide the inconsistencies and the powerlessness by always pulling on the same tired, old monkey suit.

It is only in the crisis of the lion's cage that they are forced to face the fraudulency of their true selves.

This is the reason that most teachings on the fruit of the Spirit fall dreadfully short. They usually only document what the fruit is and leave its production to the hearers. That, of course, only leads disciples into despair because, try as they might, they never seem to be able to manufacture the fruit. Resolutions and good intentions are gradually plowed under and lost.

The fruit of the Spirit, very much like nectarines and bananas, *can* be artificially duplicated to an extent. Such fruit is, however, a waxen, tasteless and un-nutritious effigy because it is what it is—manufactured, not borne. Its unreality is manifestly and nauseatingly apparent at first bite. It is only in untouched repose on the coffee table of someone's maiden aunt that ersatz bananas dare to pass themselves off as genuine. Just so, the lives of many in the Church are a constant whirl of polishing and posing—shiny, plastic apples with a dark inner reality. The genuine fruit of the Spirit is not for still life arrangements on dusty pianos. In the crucible of daily life the indwelling Holy Spirit buds, blossoms and bears the true fruit of the character of Christ.

An apple is an apple because it is the product of an apple tree. It has about it the nature of "apple-ness." The Christian life filled with the Spirit of Jesus will bear his nature in the very same way. The manner of speech, the goals, the attitudes, the longings of such a life will reveal the nature of the tree of which its fruit is borne. "Godliness" like "apple-ness" is simply the manifest witness of the character of the tree.

The fruit of the Spirit which Paul speaks of in Galatians 5 is a moral portrait of Jesus. It is absurdly futile to attempt to manufacture such fruit in one's own power even if the counterfeit could be palmed off without detection. Apart from a true baptism in the Spirit of Jesus, we are just tying wax apples on barren branches.

The great test of religion is not in merely believing God for miracles. A surge of spiritual adrenalin is often sufficient for that.

The bench mark of true holiness, on the other hand, is not gasping, "I never saw a movie," with the final death rattle.

True holiness and the fount from which flows any enduring power for ministry is simply "Christ in me, the hope of glory." Christ's joy must show in me when "sorrows like sea billows roll." Christ's love in me must keep me pleasant when my husband is an hour late for dinner and the rolls have turned to baseballs.

This will always, of course, be Christ in terms of my temperament and talents. The hope of glory is certainly "Christ in me," but it will also be Christ *as* me. Tommy Tyson once said, "We must be willing for the Holy Spirit to be as wonderfully unique in everyone else as he is in us." The Holy Spirit does not want to stamp out charismatics with cookie-cutter precision. Neither is he carving out little wooden, holiness saints standing joylessly by the door like *sanctified wooden indians*. God does not want clones of Oral Roberts, John R. Church or of anyone else. What God wants is to fully inform our humanity with the Spirit of Christ so that all the world, including boss, brother-in-law and spouse, may see Christ in us (and as us), the hope of glory.

The Cost of Pentecost

An expensive New York jewelry store displayed a fabulous collection of ornate crosses for sale. Gold, silver, bejeweled and ivory inlaid, they were also replete with fabulous price tags. Underneath was the notable announcement: *"These Crosses On Easy Terms."*

The key to Pentecostal power is upper room brokenness. Holy Spirit baptism is not for those who want stylish crosses on easy terms. To come fully alive in the supernatural power of God, one must die to the grasp of the world. That corrupting clutch of worldliness will not be shaken off easily. It is a fight to the death.

The matter is further complicated when we come to see that the triune power of evil—the world, the flesh and the devil—holds us in our own grasp. The irony of sin is that Satan's only real hope to control my life is *me*. We often labor under the misguided notion that Satan wants us to do *his* will. That is incorrect. Satan has no will in our lives. He only wants us to do *our* will.

I certainly believe in the horror of demonic activity to destroy lives. Yet I also know that God's greatest task is not to deliver me from satanic power but to pry *my* fingers off my own life. Mine enemy grows older.

One of the great modern tragedies of the church is that sad host of hopefuls traveling about from conference to conference, making annual pilgrimages to Tulsa or Bradenton or Dallas trying to "get the Holy Spirit." They are frustrated by misshapen notions of what to expect. Even more frequently, however, they are defeated in their efforts by misbegotten concepts of what is expected of *them*.

We must be reminded that God is here. He longs to fill every believer with the Holy Spirit. Before we are ever stirred to seek the gift of Pentecost, he is seeking us. The question is not whether or not we shall receive the Holy Spirit, but whether he shall receive us. God will *not* fill a vessel he does not own.

I once read an anthropological study of an ancient temple in Asia. Its altar area was literally buried under broken shards of pottery. The explanation was offered that the people in that region were pottery makers who regularly sacrificed the fruit of their craft to their god. Having created their masterpieces, that work that stood to gain them the most fame and profit, the craftsmen would take them into the temple and smash them to pieces before their stone god. The broken fragments were mute testimony that in sacrificial worship the craftsmen had given up all hope of gain from the vessel. In one shattering moment the dedicated vessel changed hands never to be reclaimed. This is the perfect picture of what Hudson Taylor called "the exchanged life." Only when I am a broken vessel on the altar of a living

God can I know the power of his life in and through me.

David Seamands once said, "We receive the Holy Spirit broken in our brokenness." I cannot, of course, know all that those words meant to him. To me, however, they seem to say that brokenness is our lot by virtue of the curse and by our own wretched sin. As long as we cling to our brokenness, owning it to ourselves, trying to impose on it some fleshly semblance of wholeness, we will never know his power. When the pride of self-ownership is broken by our brokenness and we see ourselves as we really are, we can cast the poor shards in utter self-abandonment before I AM, and he receives and restores them to wholeness. The King of all the universe says that those who offer him silver and gold shall be held in derision.

Simon, the magician in Acts 8, offered money that he also might lay his hands on and bestow the Holy Spirit. It is notable that he did not ask for the work of the Spirit in his own heart. He lusted for power in ministry, without holiness of heart. The current catastrophe in American televangelism is a modern attempt to have religious prominence and power in ministry without inner sanctity.

Peter answered Simon, "thy money perish with thee" (Acts 8:20, KJV). The more literal translation is, "to hell with you *and* your money."

Having rejected the baubles of men, God accepts what men count as useless. The King of Glory condescends to bestow his *shekinah* upon ruined broken pieces, the moment they rest on the true and living altar. "Whatever touches the altar is sanctified by the altar."

What We Do, What God Does

It seems that there are two sides to sanctification. There is that sense in which *I* sanctify myself to God. At the same time *my* dedication must be fully met by his work of grace. *He* must sanctify *me* to himself. The miracle is not that sinners cast their poor broken lives on his altar. The true miracle is rather that he receives these lives and declares them acceptable in his sight.

The few verses at the end of Zechariah are provocative indeed. They speak of a new day of holiness to be sure:

On that day HOLY TO THE LORD will be inscribed on the bells of the horses and the cooking pots in the Lord's house will be like the sacred bowls in front of the altar. Every pot in Jerusalem and Judah will be holy to the LORD Almighty (Zech. 14:20-21a).

To the ancient Jew these must have been strange words indeed. Everyone knew the sacred, golden bowls and vessels dedicated for use only in the Lord's house were not the same as a saucepan in a squalid hut. The prophet brings new light to holiness in this passage.

Holiness is not just for the "religious" parts of my life. Peeling potatoes, no less than prayer, belongs to God. Saturday night, no less than Sunday morning must bear the sacred inscription "Holy to the Lord."

Zechariah says that even the tiniest, ornamental bridle bells must be no less consecrated to God than the altar vessels. In our lives this must mean that the most peripheral, "unreligious" aspects in our lives must be as surely dedicated as our thoughts at a prayer meeting.

The frivolity of many charismatics with respect to worldliness and sensuality is an embarrassment to the whole body of Christ. It is as though they believe that if they speak in tongues, nothing else matters. It is certainly true that fish must be caught before they can be cleaned. We have all excused much in the name of the newness and the liberty of the Spirit. Now, however, it is past time that we lovingly confront some really garish inconsistencies in the body of Christ. At the risk of being accused of legalism, surely there is some way we can point out that Spirit-filled women really ought not to look like streetwalkers. Spirit-filled businessmen and attorneys cannot continue in the cut-throat ethics of the world. Immoral, materialistic slaves to fashion hardly bespeak the fruit of the Spirit of Jesus.

I have often wondered who and how many truly went to Jim Bakker and called him to accounts for *his* obvious inconsistencies. Could the tragedy have been averted by a loving rebuke? Perhaps not, but the note must be sounded none-the-less.

We cannot sanctify our hearts by changing our wardrobes or stopping tobacco use, but surely, *surely* if our hearts are clean it will finally reach our wardrobes and ambitions. What, however, can be the remotest possible rationale for "Spirit-filled" people leaving their spouses because "God doesn't want us unhappy"?! How can we justify T.V. preachers lavishing two- million-dollar homes on themselves "because God has been mighty good"?

Ironically, the holiness set has seen quite clearly the ethical side of heart holiness and often entirely missed even more profound implications. Quite frankly some of the most cold-blooded, cold-eyed, gossipy, backbiting, unloving, waspish, uncharitable people in the church are virtual holiness hounds. I have seen some folks shout, run the aisles and hold up one hand while singing old holiness hymns, only to stomp out in fury if somebody dares hold up *both* hands. *That*, it seems is charismatic! I know one well-known holiness preacher who went about behind my back trying to have me black-balled in holiness churches and camps because I was "soft on tongues." What can one suppose *that* to mean?

One well-known holiness evangelist told me "the stingiest congregations in the world are in holiness camps. They are inconsistent financially to the point of sin. They shout about missions and give pennies; they claim to be poor old folks on welfare and have thousands socked away in CD's. I'm no Pentecostal," he said, "but I wish we would give like the Pentecostals do."

Late in the last century and early in this one, many in the mainline denominations became know as "holiness fighters." Some church leaders ruined their lives and ministries opposing the holiness message. One Methodist bishop who succeeded in having a preacher stripped of his orders was later hauled off the floor of his annual conference too drunk to preside.

Now it would be an ironic tragedy if men and women who have preached holiness all their lives dissipated their ministries as "tongue-fighters." How pitiful to think of those who have claimed clean hearts coolly rationalizing their jealous hatred for charismatics.

No wonder many in the mainline denominations no longer even take the holiness message seriously. If this generation is going to experience a sustained move of the Holy Spirit it must hear a gripping message of love *and* power.

Neither loveless, holiness dogma nor flippant charismatic disregard for holy living will open the door on revival. The message for this day is nothing more or less than scriptural Christianity. It is the message of the changed heart, baptized in love, separated unto God and ministering in apostolic power! The church, the primitive, unfettered, sanctified holy church with all its graces and all its gifts intact is the only sufficient instrument of power to address this poor confused generation.

It must be clearly preached and fully experienced that tongues, interpretation, prophecy and all other gifts still belong to the church. Furthermore, they must be well irrigated by an inner well-spring of the pure, holy water of love flowing out from a sanctified heart.

The five-year-old daughter of a pastor friend of mine rushed to her father with a rosebud in hand. The pitiful little blossom was mangled beyond repair and the child's face was full of confusion.

"Why is it," she asked, holding up the poor tortured flower, "that when God opens a rose it comes out so beautiful, and when I do it, it looks like *this*?"

Then, as only a child can do, she answered her own question. "Oh, I know!" she exclaimed. "God does it from the inside!"

Pentecost Then and Now

CHAPTER VI

The Shadow of God

❖

PENTECOST AND POWER IN MINISTRY

*S*peaking as he did out of the resource of his nearly 60 years of rich experience in the church, the old priest made for a fascinating interview. Driving across the Midwest I enjoyed listening to a Catholic radio broadcast of the old warrior being gently cross-examined by a scholarly, young Jesuit. They were an interesting contrast.

One of the elder priest's more provocative stories concerned his accidentally arriving on campus at Notre Dame University on the opening night of a huge Roman Catholic charismatic conference. He described in a detached, analytical manner the things that were happening, to his obvious amazement, among the thousands of Roman Catholics gathered in a patently Catholic meeting in the very stronghold of midwestern Catholicism. My interest quickened as the older man, showing an apparent unfamiliarity, detailed some of the phenomena of the Spirit.

Finally the younger priest asked, "Father, what do you think of all this? What does it mean?"

"I don't know," was the answer, "I don't know what it means. And that's what scares me. It used to be that when I attended mass from Bangkok to Boise I knew what I would find. Now when I put my hand to the door of a Catholic Church I have no idea what will be inside. Frankly, *that* frightens me!"

I believe that old priest spoke for thousands of church folks along every point of the denominational spectrum who, sensing the obvious spiritual revolution afoot, react with fear and suspicion. That something is happening in the church today is undeniable. The dust is being shaken out of the rafters.

The contemporary movement of the Holy Spirit must be ranked as one of the three or four most significant events of American Church history. It is not my concern here to label or trace the origin of this religious revolution. The point is not whether it is called the "Charismatic Renewal" or the "Third Great Awakening." Neither am I impressed with catchy terms like "Third Wave." This move of the Spirit crosses denominational barriers and leaps national frontiers. Some claim Azusa Street as its cradle. Still others harken back to the holiness movement.

The fact is, a great longing for primitive Christianity in the power of the Holy Spirit has seized a sizable element of Christendom from Indonesia to Indiana. "Business as usual" has simply failed to meet the needs of a laity awakened to the supernatural. The increasingly strident demands of this thirsty mass have been received as adversarial by a bankrupt clergy. It is just plain confusing to many others. Some like the scribes and Pharisees react in paranoid self-preservation denouncing the whole thing as "drunken excess." Many more, like the old priest, are simply asking, "What does this mean?"

Certainly, excess is a problem in any atmosphere of revival. However the key to dealing with excess is not less of the Holy Spirit but more. It is my own observation as I have traveled and preached across many denominations all over the globe that excess is hardly the problem in most "mainline" churches. It is more nearly creeping death. Instead of trying to "rein in" a movement of God and institutionalize the life out of it, we must give the Holy Ghost his head, seeking all the while for grace to comprehend, in the light of Scripture, what God is doing.

Dr. M. G. McLuhan once said, "Our theology comes along after our experience like a little crippled dog." That is as it should be. We dare not become slaves to experience, disregarding Scripture. On the other hand, what fools we would be to ignore experiences of grace. We must receive seasons of refreshment, gladly striving less to contain them than to be pure in our hearts. Hence, what is of God will have its way in us and what is not will flow by us in the stream. If God is watering the lawn I do not want to put my foot on the hose just because a few unmannerly, neighborhood waifs cavort in the spray.

Hence it behooves us now as never before to understand the work of Pentecost. The Christian afraid of Pentecost is like a fish afraid of water or an eagle with a fear of heights. God forbid that Pentecost should ever become the exclusive property of those with the boldness to print it on the letterhead. Pentecost belongs to the whole church.

'We Thought It Was Out'

If we can come to some understanding of what God did at Pentecost, perhaps we will not react in such fear to what God is doing now. This "contemporary" move of the Holy Spirit is contemporary only in the sense that it is happening in our day.

This is not a new revival. It is not a new church, a new Spirit, a new concept, nor a new theology. There is one Lord, one faith, one baptism, one Church and one Spirit. What made us think that the 700 Club invented the Holy Ghost? What God is doing in this hour is what God did in the Upper Room.

God is still God; the Spirit remains the Spirit. And where the Church opens herself to him, the Upper Room revival will still overflow the dams of form and structure in a raging torrent of

Pentecostal power. The history of the church is a two-thousand-year-old story of the revival light of Pentecost periodically breaking through the dark mist of an apostate church.

During a series of special services at a small Northern Georgia church I stayed at the parsonage. One blustery, fall afternoon the pastor decided to burn leaves in the backyard. He refused to listen when his wife advised that this was unwise. When he set a huge tree in the backyard on fire, I knew he was in for a rugged time.

The local volunteer firemen put out the fire rather easily by amputating some of the old tree's extremities and hosing down the fallen branches. How the poor pastor suffered! Any man acting against his wife's better judgement does so only at the risk of a veritable monsoon of "I told you so's" to follow. In addition the men of that rural congregation thoroughly enjoyed the pastor's plight and happily added to verbal abuse.

Following the evening service, however, the incident took a more serious turn when the old tree suddenly blazed again. What had earlier been a fairly innocuous fire in the upper branches now became a raging conflagration that threatened the safety of the parsonage. The firemen returned this time to spray the roof of the house and take down the tree.

In response to my questions the young fireman directing the operation gave an interesting explanation of the "second" fire. It was his surmise that there was no "second" fire. Despite the pastor's subtle accusation that his wife rekindled the fire in order to keep his mistake fresh in everyone's mind, the volunteer fire chief offered the opinion that a spark from the first fire had somehow sunk into the heart of the old tree. There it lay dormant awaiting some perfect unwritten recipe of air, resin and dry tinder before bursting into view once again.

"You see, Preacher," he drawled, "they ain't been but one fire here tonight. We thought it was out, but it was just inside where we couldn't see it."

"Glory to God!" I said. "That, my friend, is the story of Pentecost."

Through long, dark nights the stately, old tree of the Church stood in picturesque powerlessness awaiting the arrival of a Martin Luther or a John Wesley or a Francis Asbury or some unsung saint in a living room prayer meeting. Then, despite petty accusations, bystanders would stare in awe at the power of a blaze they had thought was quenched and forgotten.

Easy to Miss the Essence

I am convinced that a greater understanding of what happened at Pentecost would do much to dispel the suspicion and fear concerning what is happening in this hour. What happened at Pentecost? First of all it must be remembered that what actually *happened* at Pentecost cannot be fully understood as the sum total of the *things that happened.*

The eyewitnesses of a shooting incident might each offer pertinent and correct information about the resultant noise and confusion and still leave their questioners with an utterly erroneous understanding.

"A man in a blue suit shot a man in a brown suit," one might testify.

"The man with the gun was white and the victim black," another might add.

"There were four shots fired," might seem to further clarify the murderous bloodshed.

True comprehension of the incident, however, awaits the public announcement (by some associate producer) that the whole event was staged for the filming of a new movie. What happened was *not* that shots were fired and a man fell to the pavement. What *happened* was that a movie scene was filmed.

Suppose Pat and Mike attend a football game. Upon leaving they are met in the stadium parking lot by an alien visitor from Mars or some other distant land.

"What happened in there?" the foreigner asks.

"Football," they explain.

"Yes," the visitor presses, "I understand that, but what happened?"

"Well," Mike explains patiently, "There are five men in striped shirts and billed caps. Each has a whistle and red flag. They run back and forth on a field that is 50 yards by 100 yards, madly blowing their whistles and throwing their flags in the air. If you really want to understand football, buy a striped shirt, a whistle and a flag. Run around in your yard, and whenever the fancy strikes you, blow the whistle and toss the flag in the air."

Certainly Mike is correct in that there are officials and that they throw flags around. But no description of the officials can fully describe football.

Now Pat, being of an earthy view perhaps, stares at his friend in shock. "No, no, no, Mike," Pat says, "That's not it at all. There are nine lovely little high school girls in short skirts jumping up and down on the side line . . ."

Obviously no description of the cheerleaders can fully explain the nature of the contest. In reality football simply cannot be explained in terms of its "paraphernalia." Goal posts, scoreboards, cheerleaders and referees do *not* football make.

Likewise, any attempt to understand Pentecost solely in terms of concomitant events will surely lead to error. Many things *happened* on that first Pentecost. They were exciting things! It would be a mistake to expect that *all* to happen every time Christians meet for worship. How tragic, though, to meet week after boring week in the full expectation, or even fervent hope, that none of them will happen.

Pentecost cannot be sufficiently explained only in terms of supernatural phenomena. On the other hand, we need not explain them away either. The manifestations of the Spirit must be taken for just that. They are not *what happened*, they are outward *manifestations* of what the Lord, the giver of life, was actually doing.

"What does this mean?" asked the onlookers at Pentecost.

Suppose Simon Peter had answered in terms of the manifestations. "Wind!" he might have said. "What happened was that the wind blew all through the crowd."

"Oh," someone would surely have said, "So that's all. It's nothing but a political convention!"

Or perhaps Peter might have answered, "Fire! We saw the visible presence of fire in the house!"

Then again he might have said, "We spoke in tongues! What actually happened here is that we spoke in languages that we had no natural way of knowing."

Any of the three answers would have been totally insufficient. In fact, all three combined land way short of the runway. Furthermore they not only fail to explain the Pentecostal experience, but they also leave the uninvolved onlookers utterly unconvicted of sin and of the judgment to come.

The Bottom Line of Pentecost

A charge frequently leveled at the charismatic renewal is that it has substituted temporary experience for enduring transformation. While this is certainly unfair in some ways, the extent to which it *is* true is in direct proportion to the movement's failure to articulate what *actually happens* in the Pentecostal experience.

Such a failure is disastrous. The end result will necessarily be frustrated believers discovering that their victory dissipates before the benediction. Even more calamitous for the kingdom is the horrifying spectacle of people, ministries and congregations enjoying the charismatic gifts while failing to really face and deal with the ethical inconsistency in their own lives.

Of course, the opponents of the Pentecostal message take great delight in publishing abroad the sins of charismatics. They fail to realize, of course, that the particular wickedness of some Pentecostals hardly invalidates the true experience of the Upper Room. It is a spurious implication, and the same one, in fact, made by those who dismiss all Christianity because of the Crusades in the Middle Ages or the current violence in Ireland.

The necessity remains, however, to proclaim the Pentecostal experience so clearly that it will be sought for what it really is. The balance of holiness of life and power for ministry is indispensable to any attempt to give theological expression to the deepest ministry of the Holy Spirit.

Peter's statement that, "This is that which was spoken by the Prophet Joel . . ." (Acts 2:16, KJV) was a bare expression of fact. The Holy Spirit had come. Yes! But what did it mean?

What *actually* happened at Pentecost? *The Church was born at Pentecost.* To the sound of a roaring wind, by the light of a supernatural flame a whole new reality came to be on planet earth the day that God baptized the 120 in the Holy Spirit. The new thing was a living temple, a bride and a body. This corporate being was the Church.

The Upper Room visitation, while certainly not burying the individual personalities of those present, made them deeply aware that henceforth they were part of a greater whole. Furthermore that *whole* became a living temple far fuller than the sum total of the individual bricks used.

Union With God

It is only through the power of the Holy Spirit that many can become one in Christ. The relationship between members of the church is decidedly *not* that of a bonding by subscription to commonly held convictions. Political parties and caucuses are a limited union formed across mutually important ideals or goals. Such unity may exist and excite fierce loyalty among pagan infidels. The miracle mystery of the Church finds reality only in the breath of God. Voting together is a shoddy substitute for spiritual oneness in Christ. The kingdom of God is not by acclamation. It is through crucifixion to sin and self and in resurrection by the Spirit of holiness.

The same Spirit of holiness that raised Christ Jesus from the dead, raises us up to walk in newness of life. It is not, however, an altered state. It is an exchange of breath with the very source of life. He breathes himself into me, and therein I become one with all others in whom he breathes. This union far and away transcends mere theological agreement. Because he is I AM in me, and I AM in you, we three make one. In that we live and breathe in him and he in us, the unifying of his Spirit becomes reality and that which divides is shown up for the myth it is. The Church is not a loose amalgamation of folks who have agreed to overlook their differences in order to see more evangelical Christians elected to office. The Church is a mystic, transcendent reality made manifest *in* the world, *for* the world and *to* the world. The Church is the living, breathing, walking, talking, healing, saving, delivering Body of Christ.

Hence, all theological variations on the dispensationalist anthem are paltry denials, *not* of the Holy Spirit, but of the true nature of Church. To say that miracles and gifts ceased with the apostles and "are not for this age" is to simply miss the whole point of the Church.

The Church is not just all the saved people on planet Earth at any given moment. The Church is the body of Christ! That body is the same, yesterday, today and forever. To accept a miracleless, giftless Church today is to settle for a diminished statement of who Jesus is, of what the Church is and the true nature of our unity in the Holy Ghost.

A Methodist pastor and I had an interesting exchange during a healing conference several years ago. On the second morning I entertained some questions, and he responded quickly.

"Listen, Mark," he began, "I like a lot of what you are saying. Some of this is really helpful, and I thank you. But there is one phrase you keep tossing around that really rubs me the wrong way. It's this matter of the laying on of hands. I just don't believe in that."

"Sure you do," I said. "You may not have thought of it in these terms but I know you believe in it."

He quickly bridled at this. "Wait just a minute," he said angrily. "Don't tell me what I believe! I have thought of it, and I don't like it. It smacks of arrogance and pride to think that *I* have to lay *my* hands on someone I'm asking God to heal. I don't like *that* at all. Furthermore I don't think it's Methodist."

"Aren't you a Methodist preacher?" I asked him.

"I am an ordained elder in the conference," he said stiffly.

"Who ordained you?" I asked.

"The bishop of this conference," he answered.

"How did he do it?" I asked.

"Oh, no!" he moaned.

Oh, yes! In this current outpouring of spiritual power the Church must invest itself creatively in understanding its own place in the Incarnation. The imposition of hands, like much of the rest of the ministry of power, is not a strange or unusual means or a new doctrine. On the contrary, it is an expression of a longing to bring supernatural reality to bear on traditions and formalities.

In the act of ordination the Church claims for itself the hands of Christ. "Receive thou the authority to preach the gospel and administer the sacraments," says the bishop. (Those may be United Methodist words, but the concept, if not the exact language, translates quite well across denominational boundaries.) As the bishop lays on hands, the Church is standing on the proposition that far more is involved in the act than the fingers of an elected church official. It better! Without that faith, ordination becomes nothing but the hollow ritual of dead men ordaining dead men to the ministry of death.

When the bishop (or committee of elders) lays on hands for ordination he or she does so "in the name of Jesus." The corporate hands of Christ are being stretched forth in an office of the Church. By the power of the Holy Spirit, the liveliness of Christ's body ordains his messengers for the ministry of reconciliation.

Obviously then, if Christ's body still has authority in his name to ordain, it follows that the ministry of healing and deliverance belongs to the Church now, in this age.

No Church Without The Spirit

"Where the Spirit of the Lord is there is the one true Church, apostolic and universal."

As the Church in revival power begins to take that ancient creed seriously the charismatic ministry finds a full-bodied reality. By the same token, however, where the Spirit of the Lord is *not*, there is *not* the true Church.

Apart from the Holy Spirit there is no Church. A body without breath soon becomes a corpse. The body of Christ, even while it outwardly functions, apart from the breath of God becomes a cold, dead husk. It may temporarily appear healthy to a lost world without spiritual discernment. It may even be a positive influence in the society and culture around it. Tragic confusion and bitter disillusionment will result, however, when the redemptive body of Christ becomes nothing more than a wholesome watering hole for the community of nice guys who want to sponsor Boy Scouts and coach softball teams. That is not to say that those things are sinful or that they have no business in a Church's program. It is to say that apart from the presence of the Holy Ghost the Church will lose sight of its own self-image as the supernatural body of Christ.

This is, to a great extent, responsible for the high attrition rate among modern clergy. In an age where the Church is suffering a severe identity crisis, those called to full-time ministry will be left to flounder about like beached turtles topside down on the sands of contemporaneity. Hence modern clergy are organizing neighborhood rent strikes and calling it evangelism, while trying to pep up anemic worship services with clowns and puppet shows. Far worse is the sad picture of a pitifully disoriented modern clergy descending into outright moral turpitude. This is only to be expected in a day of such "professional" confusion. When the Church is nothing more than a glorified Kiwanis Club, the clergy daily loses its soul to meaningless hospital visits, futile counseling sessions and the mad dash to get the bulletin out on Thursday. Like bored housewives in the arms of a lover, they hope to live their passionless lives above the mundane and inexplainable.

The Holy Spirit not only enlivens the Church, but he also defines the Church. To speak of a "Spirit-filled" church is to speak of a swimming fish or a breathing lung. The church apart from the dynamic, recognized, invoked presence of the Holy Ghost is a garish monstrosity. It is a ghoulish, moving corpse in a tuxedo, flaunting softball teams and men's club barbeques as proof of its liveliness, while its empty balconies, prayerless pews and powerless pulpits cry, "Death," "Death," "Death."

Casting What Kind Of Shadow?

While preaching at a large Methodist campground I took an evening stroll with my four-year-old daughter, Emily, and her slightly younger cousin, Fred. A larger than life statue of John Wesley made a great impression on them both. They stared very soberly at the great statue for a few seconds before little Fred broke the silence.

"*Who* is *that*?" he asked in revential awe.

"Don't you know who that is?" demanded my daughter with the arch superiority of a person who knows something that those around her do not. "*That* is the shadow of God!"

I remembered the passage in Acts 5 where the people brought the sick and demonized into the street when Peter passed by. As his shadow fell across them they were healed and set free. In the light of that text, I reasoned, perhaps my little daughter's answer was, in fact, a profound theological statement. John Wesley *was* the shadow of God.

So, in fact, were Peter and Paul and Martin Luther and D. L. Moody. More to the point, however, is the fact that the Church casts a shadow wherever it stands. When it remains humbly before Christ daily, being filled with His Spirit, even the Church's shadow possesses healing property. Where the Church stands confident in its own presence, its shadow is darkness only.

Wherever the Church takes on a life of its own, apart from Christ, it begins to die, and in the dying casts a pall of death on everything about it.

This is an individual truth as well as a corporate reality. Apart from the indwelling glory of Christ a man's shadow just blocks out the light. Baptized in the Holy Spirit, a river of the life of Christ flows out in healing, redemptive power from that man to all around him.

The contrast in Acts 5 between the Pharisees and the Church is stark and shocking. The Apostles laid hands on the bound and they were set free. The Pharisees laid hands on the Apostles and they were imprisoned. The Apostles offered life. The Pharisees threatened death. The Apostles were so filled with the Holy Spirit that the sick were healed. The Pharisees were so filled with indignation that they would have done murder.

Whenever voices of renewal within the Church are opposed, it is seldom on theological grounds. The basic question of the Church hierarchy is usually the very one which the Pharisees asked. "Who's in charge here anyway?" It is said of Jesus, "The common man heard him gladly." The Pharisees crucified Jesus because he threatened their position *not* their theology. In every age the Church casts a shadow. It is either the deadly shadow of a self-absorbed, paranoid, power-mad hierarchy or the healing shadow of ignorant and unlearned men who have been with Jesus.

It is hardly ever the laity who oppose a renewal in the United Methodist Church and its top-side down experience. The clergy, whose calling and vision should surely be to shake up a lethargic laity, are fighting to preserve the status quo. It is the sheep not the shepherds, which are trying to press on to higher ground. It is *always* a sign of spiritual disease when the laity in any denomination is more hungry for revival than the clergy.

What a pathetic picture when people are praying for revival, and the district superintendent, like some adolescent Barney Fife, is swaggering about with his bullet in his shirt pocket, demanding that they "act like Methodists!"

When formal religion "rises up" (Acts 5:17) all it accomplishes is to shut out the light. Where the body of Christ walks in the light its shadow heals and delivers. My old friend Tommy Tyson once said he would like to be so filled with the Holy Spirit that when he walked into a restaurant where no one knew him, people would be spontaneously healed. That is not prideful arrogance. It is the humblest hope of the Church; that the Spirit of Jesus be so glorified in us that the world around us might receive of him and not of us.

Neither is it presumptuous. We have lived in a pygmy church for so long that when we see the hope of scriptural Christianity it seems frighteningly gigantic and just a touch arrogant. The Church has often taken a "who-does-he-think-he is?" attitude toward those who dare to believe for a faith which vaguely resembles that of the early Church.

Such an attitude seems to say that such believers are taking just a little too much on themselves. That is far from true, however. The fact is that true Christian humility, while being sensitive to the utter powerlessness of humanity, is absolutely confident of God's ability to miraculously use sanctified humanity. To lose sight of that hope is to miss many of the implications of Incarnation theology, not to mention any meaningful concept of the Church as the body of Christ.

The Church, as well as all individual believers, should live in the full expectation of miracle power. In Mark 16, Jesus clearly embraces the sphere of the supernatural as the proper universe of activity for the body of believers. As the gospel is proclaimed in authority and believed in faith it is to be *expected* that signs and wonders shall follow. In the shadow of the Church shall bloom deliverance, supernatural communication, divine protection and healing.

In Acts 10:38, Simon Peter described the ministry of Jesus: "God anointed Jesus of Nazareth with the Holy Spirit and power, and how he went around doing good and healing all who were under the power of the devil because God was with him." Now shall his body do less or other than he himself? Certainly not!

He said that we would live in the expectation of partaking in His life, ministry, gifts, holiness and power. That, in fact, *is* life in the Spirit.

Notice again Acts 10:38. The verse is a clear statement of the two-fold work of the Finger of God in the life of Jesus. As Simon Peter tried to explain to a pagan household the life and ministry of Jesus, he defined the work of the Spirit of Jesus in the believer. In this one sentence we are given a terrace view on the two-fold work of the Spirit. Peter said, "God anointed Jesus of Nazareth with the *Holy Spirit* and with power."

I believe it would be a mistake to see in this a separation of baptisms. Jesus did not receive two different anointings. He did, however, receive one baptism in the Holy Spirit for holiness of life *and* power in ministry. It is this that Peter alluded in a lovely little example of parallelism to follow: ". . . who went around doing good *and* healing all who were under the power of the devil."

What Happened At Pentecost

At first glance, that sentence may seem forced. I believe, however, that the power of Peter's declaration that Jesus "went around doing good" did not escape Cornelieus, a Roman soldier surrounded by an empire of men doing evil. In modern English the occasional "doing good" has come to mean hardly more than performing acts of beneficence. It seems clear, however, that Peter meant much, much more. The fact that Jesus did many good things would seem hardly worth mentioning. Peter must have meant that he was, and did, exclusively good.

That is as simple a statement of Christ's holiness of nature as can be found, if it is taken literally. Many do good. Only he does only good because he is only good.

Peter then added, ". . . and healing all who were under the power of the devil."

In other words Jesus did good *and* healed. This certainly cannot mean that healing was not doing good. I believe the most appropriate conclusion is that Peter was speaking of living in holiness *and* ministering in supernatural power.

That is the hope of the Church as well because we are his body filled with his breath. What happened at Pentecost, the glib have explained, is that people spoke in tongues.

No! No! A thousand times no!

What happened at Pentecost is that God proved that the sanctified heart and miraculous ministry of the Word could find incarnate reality in the corporate body of the Church. That resulted in supernatural communication. Tongues were a manifestation of that power. So was the authority of Peter's Pentecostal sermon. There were also awesome demonstrations of deliverance, divine protection and healing.

We are not to presume that all of the signs of Mark 16 occur every time every local body meets. The benighted lot keeping rattlesnakes under the pulpit, far from having more faith than others, actually demonstrate their inability to trust God with his Church *and* his universe at the same time. Unable to rest confidently in the knowledge that God will richly supply miracles of his protection when they are needed, they have decided to "force God's hand" in Cleopatran taffy-pulls. They have so put themselves in the picture that, far from being a miracle presence in the world, they cast an ominous shadow of dangerous, evil pride.

CHAPTER VII

A Kiss and a Hug

❖

ONE SPIRIT, TWO WORKS

*S*uppose the onlookers at Pentecost had pressed Peter for further explanation. Suppose someone had said, "Yes, fine, so the Church has come to be. So what? What we want to know is what, if anything, has happened to *you*?" Was what happened at Pentecost a corporate reality only? Or did something happen in Peter and the others, as individuals, that found a corporate expression?

This is an important question. If the Church enjoys *only* corporate life, Pentecost as a personal experience of grace may be unnecessary for all subsequent generations of the members of the body. If the body of Christ receiving its breath of power for ministry experienced no definable work in the individuals at Pentecost, then there should be no serious expectation of its repetition. In this way of thinking Pentecost becomes a "once and never again" event.

On the other hand, if something happened in each of the 120 as individual members of the body of Christ, then every member, until Jesus' return, might well hope for his or her own personal Pentecost. The Church might, as an ongoing corporate body, receive the Holy Spirit once and for all. The Church lives on. Simon Peter, the man, does not. He will never be repeated. Whatever the Holy Spirit did in *him* as an individual at Pentecost must be done again and again and again in every other individual added to the body.

Perhaps a bit more subtle is the svelte suburban set who, laughing at those misguided fools, fall to exactly the same sin themselves. Not daring to trust God with his Church and the universe, they also are going to "force God's hand." By fleshly formalism in worship and stupefying preachments on the "errors of the charismatic movement" they hope to keep God silent and miracleless. On the other hand the "rattlesnake" set are trying to *make* God act. The pastel pink, nervous evangelicals at First Church are trying to preclude his doing anything not printed in the bulletin.

The Possibility of Personal Pentecost

Pentecost was God's witness to the world that his own incarnate testimony was to continue. Jesus' ascension to his heavenly throne was not the end of God's sight, the Church rose up in the world's sight. Endued with the Spirit of Jesus, ministering in his love and power, and casting his shadow, the Church—the real Church—is not ecclesiastical office holders or pastors who have become clerks.

The Church is alive wherever the oil of Pentecost fuels the flame of God's testimonial lamp stand. Wherever man-made substitutes are burned on gilded altars the suffocating stench of scorched plasticity replaces the sweet-smelling savor of incense.

Philip of Macedonia secured the greatest mind of his day to tutor his son Alexander. What better preparation for a future monarch than to be taught by Aristotle himself? Before he was 30 Alexander had a lifetime of victories under his belt. He extended his empire with a formidable display of military prowess and soon became the world's best known man.

Early in his meteoric career he visited Corinth, where a congress of the Greek city-states was meeting. During the course of his visit Alexander, who put a high value on philosphers and ideas, went to see Diogenes of Sinope. He found the old philosopher basking in the sun.

The king, who was in the process of conquering the known world with all its riches, the ruler who put personal fame and pride above every other consideration, greeted the older man and asked whether he could do anything for him. After all, there were very few limits.

But when he offered the world, Diogenes merely replied, "Yes. You can stand a little to one side out of my sun" (*The Age of Alexander*, a collection of Plutarch's work, Penguin Books, 1973, pg. 266).

The world stares toward the Church with pathetic longing. Wherever the Church stands in prideful, parochial, self-absorption, obsessed with its own little universe of accomplishments, it succeeds only in blocking the light of Christ and casting a shadow of putrefying gloom. From its knees, in humble repentance, pleading for Pentecostal power in place of professionalism, the Church casts the shadow of God. Around its edge the poor, sick, demonized world, languishing in darkness, will find light and healing.

Now the question remains, what *did* the Holy Spirit do in Peter? What does he do in any believer? (Acts 15:7). Attempting to construct some rationale for his water baptizing of Gentiles (Acts 10), Peter appealed to higher authority. His argument was, "If God gave them the Holy Spirit, who was I to withhold water?"

Then, as if to defuse the situation he apparently answered one implied question before it could be asked, "How do you know they received?"

Peter's answer has nothing to do with gifts or tongues or any other outward sign. He says, "God, who knows the heart, showed that he accepted them by giving the Holy Spirit to them, just as he did to us. He made no distinction between us and them, for he purified their hearts by faith" (Acts 15:8-9).

Any serious attempt to arrive at a biblical theology of the Holy Spirit must give special consideration to these two verses. "Giving the Holy Spirit to them, just as he did to us . . ." By using the word "us" Peter obviously spoke as a veteran of Pentecost to fellow veterans, just as he obviously felt that what had happened in Cornelius' house had been a true Pentecostal experience. It did not seem particularly remarkable to Peter or the others that the Pentecostal blessing had been experienced by others than themselves. A Pentecostal outpouring subsequent to their own Upper Room experience had been previously witnessed by James and John at Samaria. This was noteworthy only because those at Cornelius' house were Roman Gentiles.

Peter made it clear (as if it were not already clear enough) at the Jerusalem conference that the Pentecostal experience was not an historical landmark to be looked back upon and relished vicariously by future generations of believers. Holy Spirit baptism had been received *personally* by many who were added to the body of Christ after the Upper Room Pentecost.

God, being no respecter of persons, made no difference between Jews and Gentiles, generations, sexes or cultures. The Upper Room transcends its own historicity. Certainly the Church was baptized there! Simon Peter, however, was also baptized there. So were the Samaritans in Acts 8, the Ephesians in Acts 19, and the Romans in Cornelius' house in Acts 10.

They *personally* went to the Upper Room. It was not just somehow tucked into the package of becoming a believer. They all personally experienced some real inner work of Pentecost. Every new believer in every generation and society is called to that same Upper Room experience. Peter said that God gave the Gentiles at Cornelius' house the Holy Ghost just as he did to Peter himself, James, John and all the others at Pentecost.

The corporate Church body will find Pentecostal revival when individual Christians again believe for a personal baptism in the Holy Ghost. When believers are not called to the Upper

Room, taught to expect, urged to tarry and admonished to receive *personally*, the Church flounders in embarrassing impotence.

The Church will never utterly disappear. God will preserve a remnant against the gates of hell. It is a disastrous mistake, however, to believe that the health and vitality of the Church in any age can be somehow separate from the lives of believers. To assume that, because the Lord has vouchsafed the protection of his Church, all believers in any age are somehow automatically Spirit-baptized, is to court a season of useless existence. Existence is not the point. The Church will *be* when Jesus returns. The point is rather that the *state* of the Church can not be disassociated from the condition of the individual lives that fill the pulpits and pews.

Two Works of Grace

I heard a radio preacher declare, "All this seeking the Holy Spirit business is useless. Every Christian since the day of Pentecost has had the Holy Spirit. They're seeking something they already have."

Certainly there is a sense in which that is absolutely correct. No one can even *be* a Christian apart from the Holy Spirit. By the same token, a strong point can be made that the Holy Spirit is active upon a life even *before* salvation for the work of conviction.

The fact remains, however, that *something* happened at Pentecost. A corporate experience was certainly shared. Just as certainly the individuals there knew something had *happened* in them personally. To deny that is to deny Peter's own testimony in Acts 15:8-9. To affirm it is to open the door of the Upper Room for all successive generations of Christians.

Perhaps there is some help for those who are nervous at calling individuals to a personal Pentecost if we consider the vocabulary more carefully. The experience of Pentecost is variously referred to in Scripture and the writings of the saints of the Church.

John the Baptist used the phrase "baptized with the Holy Spirit and with fire" (Luke 3:16). The point could be made that he spoke of Pentecost alone except for all the subsequent chapters of Acts in which new believers (even Gentiles) found the Pentecostal experience personally.

Jesus used the same terminology in Acts 1:5. These two must have implied some kind of "washing" concept by the phrase. It is difficult to imagine what they might have meant apart from the classical idea of cleansing. Hence a personal work is necessitated. It is obviously impossible to cleanse *all* of a group of anything, from pigs to people, and not cleanse each one.

The apostle Paul used the phrase "receive the Holy Spirit" in Acts 19:1-2. He cannot have meant that some "have" the Holy Spirit and some do not. There must have been relational distinction involved. He must have meant *something* by "receive the Holy Spirit." He was speaking of receiving the same Holy Spirit previously known, in a new way, a new level of relational activity.

In his Acts narratives Luke, the beloved physician, uses a variety of phrases to refer to a personal Pentecost. In Acts 8 he uses two. In verses 15 and 17 he employs the Pauline phrase "receive the Holy Spirit." But in verse 16 he says, "because the Holy Spirit had not yet come upon any of them; they had simply been baptized into the name of the Lord Jesus." Now it is quite simply insufficient to argue that what happened in verse 17 was that the Samaritans actually became Christians. These were folks who had publicly become water-baptized believers *before* Peter and John ever arrived. By the Holy Spirit of conviction and faith they had come to believe. When Peter and John arrived, they did *not* pray that these might become believers. They prayed that they might "receive the Holy Spirit."

Certainly the Holy Spirit had been active in them for conviction and saving faith. Luke could not have meant that they had no relationship with the Holy Spirit. He clarifies it with "be-

cause the Holy Spirit had not yet *come upon* any of them . . ."
Luke surely spoke of a *new* level of activity by the Spirit; that
is, something not done, not someone unknown. Jesus had already said it in John 14:17, "The Spirit of truth . . . the world
cannot accept him, because it neither sees him nor knows him.
But you know him, for he lives with you and will be in you."

The argument that Christians need not receive the Holy
Spirit because they already know him seems specious indeed in
the face of the Lord's words here. Only those who know him
and recognize his presence *with* them are candidates to receive
the Holy Spirit *in* them. This is far more than prepositional gym-
nastics. Jesus was a master economist of words. He was showing, first, that receiving the Holy Spirit is not for unbelievers.
Furthermore, He was demonstrating that believers are not going
to be baptized in a new Spirit. Instead they are to receive a new
work done by the Spirit they already know.

I find the classical Wesleyan terminology especially helpful
at this point. The Wesleyans speak of a *second work of grace*.
John Wesley used *grace* interchangeably with the *Holy Spirit*.
Therefore, Wesley speaks of two works of the Holy Spirit. Many
who are doubtful that receiving the Holy Spirit is for those who
are already saved, might be helped to realize that it is not a matter of receiving a Spirit which they feel they already have. It is
receiving a *work* not already done.

By the time Joshua assembled the people of Israel on the
banks of the Jordan, a whole generation had died in the wilderness. God never planned such a catastrophe. "Plan A" was for
Israel to leave Egypt, receive the Law at Sinai and move straight
into Canaan. The generation of Moses that had been delivered
from Egypt was the very generation God intended to possess the
Promised Land. In cowardice and unbelief they died in wretched
failure, leaving the prize to the future.

In Joshua 3:1-5 is found the perfect Old Testament image of
two works of grace. Israel is the Church and every believer in
particular. Joshua is the leader, deliverer, savior—if you will, a
type of Jesus. The two miraculous crossings, the Red Sea and

the Jordan, express two works of grace.

In all the pages of the Old and New Testaments, Egypt is consistently an expression of the life of sin and bondage. Through the Red Sea of Jesus' blood we pass to freedom. It is a work of grace, in that we do not deserve it, help it or fully comprehend it even as we receive it. The Hebrew slave huddling in his hut crying out in groanings of his soul for deliverance for himself and his family never dreamed what lay ahead. Never in his wildest fancies did he visualize the return of Moses or the plagues or the cleaving of the waters. These things were planned in the counsels of heaven and executed in history without his assistance. Amazing grace!

Across the Red Sea and the Jordan

By faith we receive the atoning work of Calvary. The blood of Jesus gains for us mercy and eternal life. Salvation, assurance, forgiveness, justification, regeneration, adoption are all words used to mean the same thing. It is the first of two landmark crises of spiritual experiences. Generally and commonly this experience is known as being "saved." It is simply trusting, by faith, in a work already done by God to secure for us a right standing with him and the implanting of his life where there was death. Being "born again" by faith is the *first work of grace*, which is signified by the Red Sea crossing.

Can we think for one moment that the pitiful Hebrew slave, having been miraculously redeemed from Egypt's hand, was destined for a wretched death in the desert? No! The land of milk and honey lay before him. That son of Abraham was not brought out of Egypt to meander through the wilderness for 40 years. While he slept in his slave's hovel, God broke Egypt and then parted the sea before him. All that was not done for him to inherit the sands of the Sinai. He was supposed to be "bound for the promised land." A second miraculous crossing at Jordan's banks was his for the asking. Lightly regarded and easily rejected, this blessing awaited the claiming by his son's generation. That second crossing at the Jordan was also a work of grace. Subsequent to his crossing the Red Sea for salvation from Egypt's living death, God longed to take the ex-slave across Jordan to rest in a land prepared for him. God offered, not only freedom, but a place, a possession, an inheritance!

In New Testament terms, that second work of grace, that Canaan experience, is *Pentecost.* In the Upper Room those who had crossed over out of death into life found the power of life. The folks in the Upper Room were not unsaved people who found salvation. They were saved people, among whom were the apostles, and they found the promised possession of Pentecost. The crossing of the Jordan in no way invalidated the crossing of the Red Sea. By no means! The former was necessary to the latter and the latter was the fulfillment of the former.

The need for a personal Pentecost does not denigrate the efficacy of the salvation experience. That radio evangelist who rants, "When I got saved I got it *all,*" misses the point. He has failed to hear Caleb and Joshua proclaim, "There's more." Caleb never dreamed that any expression of the necessity to cross Jordan would be perceived as ingratitude for God's earlier deliverance at the Red Sea.

Yet with the fulfillment of the Promised Land within sight, Israel chose to turn back into the desert. How utterly tragic is the decision, at any crisis point, to receive less than God offers. The Christian who turns back at the point of Pentecost is settling for the desert within.

The unmitigated pathos of the Hebrew's choice of death in the desert over life in Canaan must find explanation somehow. Part of the answer, of course, is in their craven responses to the spies' report. The land of milk and honey was also, it appeared, the land of Jericho and giants. Many believers reconnoiter life in the Spirit and, deciding it is only for the Samuel Chadwicks and George Muellers, turn back in weak resignation to meander in the wilderness of half-hearted religion.

Upon seeing the book, *Giant Steps*, on my desk, a young

man said to me, "That book's not for me. My legs are too short."
There are some formidable fortresses to take and some foes that
must be fought to fully possess the land. Paranoid preoccupa-
tion with the hurdles to sanctified living fails to take into account
what Caleb said, "If the Lord is pleased with us, he will lead us
into that land . . . and will give it to us. . . . The Lord is with us.
Do not be afraid of them" (Numbers 14:8-9).

In other words, to opt for the desert is self-centered religion;
"*I* will fall." That is *not* faith in God. We have no idea of God's
helping grace on the near side of Jordan. On the far side of full
surrender (and the baptism in the Holy Spirit) after the crossing,
everything is different. *We* are changed. The Holy Spirit has
entered the picture in a whole new and powerful way. The walls
of Jericho will not seem quite so impregnable on the sunny banks
of full deliverance. After the baptism at Jordan, God will grant
streams of victory which we cannot know as we struggle to free
ourselves from the reality of our disobedience. When the
succeeding generations finally did cross over, Jericho proved to
be the least of their troubles. Hear the Word of the Lord, "How
long will they refuse to believe in me, in spite of all the
miraculous signs I have performed among them?" (v. 11).

To refuse to receive the baptism in the Holy Spirit is not
merely to elect a snug little niche for folks with "short legs." It
is to limit the holy one of Israel. It is to despise all the miraculous
keeping power of God. It is, furthermore, to rebelliously risk
losing all in the desert. God said, "I will strike them down with
a plague and destroy them . . ." (v. 12). Pentecost is *not* optional
equipment. The full blessing of Canaan-rest does not mean that
the salvation experience at the Red Sea was insufficient or lacking. It is rather that they are *two distinct works* of the Finger of
God. The one must necessarily be subsequent to the other, just
as it is impossible to cross two bodies of water simultaneously.
Although separation in time may be so abruptly abbreviated as
to make them so appear. However, as in the physical realm, each
crossing affords a different shoreline.

Hugging and Kissing

Many ask, "Cannot salvation and baptism in the Spirit occur at once?" The answer is, "Of course." The obvious example occurred at Cornelius' house in Acts 10. The point remains, however, that two works were done. I present one earthy analogy, praying to bring no offense with it. A kiss and a hug may be enjoyed at once, to be sure. In fact that is an extremely gratifying way to do it, in my judgment. Yet, even if enjoyed at the same time, the most inexperienced lad knows the difference in the two.

Many years ago when I was pastoring in north Georgia my wife announced one Saturday that we simply had to drive into downtown Atlanta to the S & H center to cash in some trading stamps. This was a dismal prospect indeed. In addition to three hours of driving in city traffic, it meant trifling away a creative and imaginative Saturday afternoon stretched out on the sofa watching football. Arriving at the "green stamp store" in a suitable huff, I was thrilled to see the sign over the entrance: Redemption Center. Inside we found "our" purchase, a lamp. I was utterly disgusted. A lamp! What a pedestrian waste! *I* wanted a toy, an electronic gadget, something *fun*. Furthermore, I thought the lamp looked like it was stolen from a cheap motel.

Surrendering the required stamps we redeemed the lamp. We rescued it from the wicked old S & H people, and that at no small cost. It took the time, the football game, a lazy afternoon, the gasoline *and* the trading stamps. Having redeemed the ugly thing at so dear a cost, do you suppose that I left it on the sidewalk outside and drove off? Certainly not! I took it home. I did not just redeem it *out* of the S & H center; I redeemed it unto myself. I gave it a resting place of my choosing, not just a precarious street corner liberty from the bondage of the market place.

In the same way God did not just rescue the Hebrews from Egypt. He brought them out by one work of grace that they might, by another, possess an inheritance of rest. The baptism in the Holy Spirit is the doorway to second rest, holiness of heart and peace within. We are not destined for the nomadic, directionless, purposelessness of the soul's desert. We are children of a mighty King. He has prepared a possession for us in Canaan, if we will only arise and take the land.

For many years I preached what I thought was the gospel while it was only forgiveness. That, of course, is no mean blessing. It is, however, less than God prefers. The idea that God, at so great a price as the cross, would redeem a soul from hell and not provide victory over sin is contrary to Scripture. Calvary justifies a man. Pentecost sanctifies him. Peter said, "their hearts were *purified by faith.*"

The outpouring of the Holy Spirit in the Upper Room was more than an en masse empowerment of the Church as a body. It was an experience of inner cleansing for each one personally. In the very moment that the Church burst into flame, each person present was sanctified and empowered for ministry. Believers longing for a distinct victory draw scant comfort from pastoral pontifications that the "Church received the Holy Spirit at Pentecost." The people are hungry and they know it; they are thirsty and will not be assuaged with cold lectures on historical landmarks.

Imagine the excitement a man might know upon being informed that he was being given a new house. How his eagerness to occupy it would grow as the features and furniture are glowingly described to him. "I will move in today!" he might exclaim with genuine enthusiasm.

"No, no," comes the answer. "That will never do! This is a *very* stable and sedate neighborhood. Your moving in would cause quite an unsatisfactory stir. You might even become excited. God forbid! This neighborhood finds those types of emotional experiences distasteful. No, no. Moving in will not be acceptable here. Just *live* in it. It is yours, after all. But no moving in allowed!"

"How can I *live* in a house into which I have never moved initially?" he might well ask in confusion.

"*That* is your problem," comes the callous answer. "If you figure it out, though, you will *love* the house."

Much of what passes for holiness preaching does little more than bring bitter frustration upon the heads of hungry believers. Describing life in the Spirit in alluring detail does little to facilitate victory in the life of the Christian if the way in is veiled in homiletical mumbo-jumbo and camp meeting jargon.

Preaching on the meaning of Pentecost must include clear enunciation of *how* to be *personally baptized in the Holy Spirit* as well as *what* life in the Spirit is like. The Word of God is an open door on Pentecost. Will modern preachers manage to hide what the Lord himself has been trying to reveal for 2,000 years?

How to Receive Him

What happened at Pentecost is that the Church was born into the world in wind and flame even as individual believers were sanctified and empowered for service. The full blessing of Pentecost, the two-fold work of the Finger of God for holiness and power, is available to every believer who will draw nigh with faith.

A crowd of curious, country onlookers watched a group of men scurrying about the strange contraption in the pasture. It was the early 1900s and they were seeing their very first airplane.

One elderly skeptic loudly prophesied failure. "It'll never fly! They ain't gonna get 'er up!"

As its owners manipulated the strange machine toward the open field, the old farmer continued his negative harangue. Finally the engine roared to life and the prop whirred into a blur.

"I don't care," the bumpkin continued, "that thing won't never, ever fly!"

The rickety biplane bounced down across the pasture, leapt into the air and soared gracefully above the tree tops. After a moment, all eyes turned on the man, awaiting his admission.

"Well," he said, "if they're gonna do it *that* way—"

Often people have little faith in even the greatest of theological principles because they cannot see how to get the contraption in the air. It is one thing to lend assent to the doctrine of Holy Spirit baptism; it is quite another to actually receive it. Many seekers live frustrated lives at this point because they do not know what to do, what to expect nor how to pray.

There are some ways to prepare to receive. First, several questions must be asked.

1. *Are you born again?* Only if you answer "yes" may you continue in hope. This is a gift for *believers*. If you are a saved Christian, proceed.

2. Are you willing to crown Jesus "Lord" in every area of your life? Are you content for him to own your pride, possessions, family, fortune, future and your sinful ego?

3. *Do you believe the promise of the Holy Spirit is for you?* Take a second and read Luke 11:13 once again. "If you then, though you are evil, know how to give good gifts to your children, how much more will your Father in heaven give the Holy Spirit to those who ask him!"

Do you need to be in some special place? My precious friend, Terry Teykl, tells of a time in his life when he sought the baptism diligently. He hungrily attended conferences and conventions everywhere seeking the blessing. One day his teen-aged daughter received the baptism while vacuuming the church carpet! Terry said that he nearly wore out the pile, vacuuming that carpet over the next few weeks. We often think the baptism will come in some special place. I received it in a hotel ballroom. My mother was in a pick-up truck, my father in his backyard and my wife at the altar of a Methodist church! If God is no respecter of persons, surely he is no respecter of places. You can receive *right where you are this very minute.*

When is the best time to receive the Holy Spirit? The time is when you can no longer live, minister, teach, preach or pray without him. Believers do without the Holy Spirit because they are content to. Time? When any desperate soul says, "Now, God oh now, fill me now!" That is the perfect time.

How? Fall on your knees and pray. Earnestly pray a prayer something like this:

Lord Jesus, I know that I am a Christian. But I confess to you my need for this baptism. Sanctify my unclean heart. Empower me for service.

Lord, I am so hungry. I am so thirsty. Fill me now, I implore you, according to Luke 11:13. I cannot let you go until you fill me. Come, come Holy Spirit—fill me just now in Jesus' Name.

Now, quickly—do not hesitate—close your eyes, lift your hands and begin to praise Jesus out loud. Do not worry about your words. Just release your spirit in praise. Let if flow out.

In the Name of Jesus—
RECEIVE THE HOLY GHOST!
Now let your praises flow. Close this book now. Close your eyes. Praise God your sanctifier. The Comforter has come!

CHAPTER VIII

The Hair of the Dog

❖

LIFE IN THE SPIRIT

Among the onlookers at Pentecost were a few of those particularly doubtful skeptics who dismissed the Upper Room fireworks as common drunkenness. The ever astute Simon Peter refuted this claim with a brilliant stroke of complex apologetics. He pointed out the impracticability of getting 120 men, women and young people falling down, babbling drunk before nine o'clock in the morning.

This metaphor was not totally wasted however. In a way, those in the Upper Room were "under the influence." Filled with the Holy Spirit, they were swept up in a power beyond themselves or beyond anything they had previously known. They had imbibed of the new wine of the kingdom.

Paul embroidered on this same theme in Ephesians 5:18 when he said, "Do not get drunk on wine, which leads to debauchery. Instead, be filled with the Spirit."

Paul sees some comparison and contrast between life lived

in the Spirit and drunkenness. As the alcohol content in the blood rises it alters the personality. A person may feel a temporary wave of happiness as it is absorbed through the capillaries. Often there is a heightened sense of well-being and confidence as the warm glow of alcoholic euphoria blurs the definitions of reality.

The Holy Spirit works rather like that, only in reverse. As the Spirit of holiness begins to penetrate the mind, spirit and body, reality is brought into its proper eternal perspective. As the warping of sin that twists and distorts life is suddenly struck away, the soul exults at its new-found liberty like a leap to hyperspace. Inebriated on truth, the unfettered soul soars in ever-widening circles of praise, finding expression in gifts and graces heretofore hidden in the mists of bondage.

Is it any wonder that the observers at Pentecost ascribed the exuberance of the believers to drunkenness? They *were* drunk! The Spirit of light had suddenly banished the darkness. The lines of life were suddenly brought into shocking clarity. Without warning, the dullness of a half-life was replaced with a landscape blindingly illumined with the brilliance of ultimate reality.

One of my sweetest and clearest recollections immediately following my own experience of the baptism in the Holy Spirit is of a certain early morning stroll just a few days later. I recall how the trees and lawns seemed so green and the sky a blue I had never seen before. The whole world appeared as if it had been recently hosed down. The air seemed pollutionless and, well, "dust free."

In actuality it was I not the world which had changed. The dirty film over my own soul had been peeled away. The fresh clean air of reality was sparkling wine. I had to fight an urge to giggle at absolute nothing. Drunk! And very nearly disorderly!

I have often heard it said that, when a hangover follows drunkenness, many prescribe some of "the hair of the dog that bit you." They say one should drink a little more of whatever was drunk in excess the night before. Now I cannot say that I have ever heard a "Holy Spirit hangover," but I can at least see something of a similarity.

I have heard some speak of a "crash" or "burn-out" after the baptism in the Spirit. They refer to those desert seasons in the life of the Spirit-filled believer when the music grows faint and the dancing awkward and a bit forced. The "flow" of Pentecost may seem to have gone dry. *That* is when the only suitable prescription is "the hair of the dog."

Paul told the Ephesians (5:18), "Do not get drunk on wine . . . be filled with the Spirit." The Greek tense employed might more nearly (apart from its awkwardness in English) have been translated, ". . . be being filled." In other words, live constantly receiving the Holy Spirit. An earthier wisdom might say, "If you want to stay drunk, you have to keep drinking."

Unless both the crises *and* the process of life in the Spirit are emphasized, the result will be imbalance, inconsistency and frustration. Certainly it is impossible to dwell in a house not initially occupied. By the same token, immaturity, futility and even sin will dog those who fail to see past the crisis point of baptism in the Spirit.

A famous sculptor was once asked how, out of a shapeless, formless block of granite, he could create a statue of a horse so lively that it appeared as if it might gallop away at any moment.

"It is quite easy," he replied, "I simply take my hammer and my chisels and chip away everything that does not look like a horse."

That is the ongoing work of the Holy Spirit in the life of the believer. The Holy Spirit must chip away everything that does not look like Jesus. Certainly a great deal is instantly accomplished in the moment of Holy Spirit baptism. It goes without saying, of course, that the whole *life* is staked out as the property of Jesus.

It must be remembered, though, that much remains to be done. The habits of holiness are very important. Prayer, the constant study of the Word, praise and public worship are means of grace. Unceasing prayer is the "hidden hip flask" of a Spirit-filled Christian. In his pocket testament the believer can steal a "nip" between classes or at his lunch break.

Immaturity Not the Spirit's Doing

With regard to the gifts of the Spirit, it must be remembered, as Paul said in 1 Cor. 12, that we are not mindless pagans writhing in idolatrous ecstasy and "led astray" by religious experience. That inspires sensual euphoria. Pentecostal "drunkenness" does not create babbling maniacs careening through "spiritual" contortions over which they have no control. "The spirits of prophets are subject to the control of prophets" (1 Cor. 14:32).

Loose talk about the gift of tongues has been particularly destructive in this regard. One otherwise reasonable translation of the New Testament even renders the Greek references to the gift of tongues as "tongues of ecstasy." Nothing could be further from the truth. Unthinking charismatics have not helped by saying things like, "I had no control over it. I was just caught up in the Spirit and began to speak in tongues and just couldn't stop even though I knew many there might be offended."

What drivel! The Finger of God is not doing pre-frontal lobotomies on believers, turning them into irresponsible automatons. Along with the supernatural empowerments, he brings the wisdom, maturity, graciousness and sensitivity to use them in a controlled, orderly and edifying way. "Under the influence" of the Holy Spirit, the charismata in the life of the believer become beautiful manifestations of the supernatural power of God to bless, heal and instruct. "Drunk on the flesh," they become an ax and crowbar applied to a tea room with the delicacy of a Neanderthal.

Much irresponsibility and sloth has been blamed on the Holy Spirit. Immature Christians who summarily quit jobs, make foolish business transactions and say hurtful, wounding things while claiming the guidance of the Holy Spirit do more damage than they can imagine.

All too often when a believer says, "I felt led by the Spirit," he or she assumes a kind of arrogant impregnability that presumes upon the humility of others. No right-thinking Christian wants to stand in the way of God! Hence wiser, more mature voices are often drubbed into cowed silence by Spirit-filled folks who are operating in fleshly pride rather than "being filled."

It is much easier to be a card-carrying charismatic than it is to "be being filled." The only way to insure that the gifts of the Spirit in our own lives are constantly informed by love, humility and wisdom is to keep soaking them in prayer. The pitiable paranoia in much of the Church, with regard to the exercise of the biblical gifts, is atrocious. It is, however, only aggravated by charismatic will-o'-the wisps obsessed with *ministry in the Spirit.*

In a recent conference I shared the platform with a "leader" in the charismatic movement. An hour into the service he made his dramatic entrance. (Is "ministry in the Spirit" the main act to be trotted out only after the band has whipped the crowd into a frenzy?) His gold bracelet and diamond rings flashed in the spotlight. Waving a dollar bill under his nose he called out, "Everybody repeat after me, 'Sweet smelling money'!" Then after the sermon he offered up "words of knowledge" which seemed forced and obligatory at best. The entire evening seemed fake. Its side-show fanfare seemed more akin to the lights on Broadway than to the shadow of God.

The complicating factor in all this is that many can readily testify to having found salvation and healing in just such meetings. God will move where there is faith. I must quickly add that I have personally been blessed in some really brassy services. Such services must not blind us to what is real and paralyze our ministries simply because they embarrass us. Misuse of the gifts hardly invalidates their reality. This is not a plea for the stolid conservatism of tight-collar evangelicalism. Far from it! Christianity is no more effective when its petticoats are starched. I am not suggesting some particular style of ministry. Neither floodlights nor chandeliers avail anything. In fact, just the opposite is true. The gifts of the Spirit are seen to their most genuine advantage in ministries which are less preoccupied with style and image and more concerned with content and reality. The minister who is daily seeking to cultivate the presence and person of the Holy Spirit is most likely to know the reality of consistent, genuine charismatic ministry. Those attempting to surround themselves in an aura of charismatic mystique while neglecting the habits of personal holiness may find miracles in ministry and heartbreak in divorce court. The heart, which each day presents itself to the Finger of God and prayerfully pleads for a fresh inscription of holiness unto the Lord, is the heart that will cast a whole shadow. The life "being filled" is the life that volitionally, intentionally, regularly draws on the wells of devotion in the secret place with Jesus. The minister who drinks deeply, daily of the Spirit of Jesus reflects the wholeness of Christ's person, as well as the power of our Lord's ministry.

The rhinestone cowboy, drunk on popularity, gradually becomes a husk of a minister; he becomes a compromised stage-image, living in splintered separation from the private reality of his own soul. Performance-oriented Christianity breeds scandal and broken marriages.

It furthermore accords automatic credence to voices of dubious merit simply on the basis of talent. As a result, we have the sad spectacle of popsingers barely out of their teens, wearing skin-tight jeans and dancing suggestively to "Christian" lyrics while making mindless, cotton-candy, religious pronouncements. The Christian talkshows confer on them an immediate, honorary doctorate in "successful Christianity" as soon as they sell a million albums. An over-emphasis on sales instead of souls creates an unfortunate "star system" of Christianity which eventually finds itself in the awkward situation of making allowances for its stage idols. The "star mentality" maintains that the celestial beings of the silver screen are not quite subject to the same moral laws as the rest of us. That thinking has definitely invaded the Christian TV realm.

Discipleship Is the Key

When the 70 returned to Jesus bubbling with reports of miracles of healing and deliverances, Jesus responded with a cryptic reference to Satan. "I saw Satan fall like lightning from heaven" (Luke 10:18). It seems to be the popular understanding that Jesus was rejoicing with them in their demonstration of the ministry of power. Perhaps. Certainly Jesus' victory over Satan is to be manifested in miracles in and through his Church. In the light of the context, however, I am convinced that Jesus was making a far deeper response. Certainly the Lord was pleased with their thrilling stories of supernatural ministry. They were doing *only*, exactly what he had sent them to do. We must still be about the ministry of healing, declaration and deliverance. Listen, though, to our Lord's caution to his disciples who were empowered for ministry.

"Remember, even before you were born, before the earth was old I saw the heavenly revolt. I saw the son of the morning, the most beautiful archangel who waited before the Father's glory. I saw Lucifer. I saw him robed in a loveliness you have never imagined and endued by God with a marvelous richness and diversity of gifts. I saw him begin to take personal pride in the handiwork of God, until rebellion cracked the universe at the seams. And I saw him fall from heaven like a bolt of lightning, never again to minister before God but bound forever in the hellish work of self-consumed but supernatural ministry" (author's paraphrase of Luke 12).

Could it be that the memory of this very admonition beckoned the apostles to their life of devotion (Acts 3:12-13)? Far from denying their miraculous ministry of healing, deliverance and public evangelism, they affirmed it and exercised the awe of all Jerusalem. How could they deny that remarkable morning of glorious "drunkenness"? Never! Instead, setting about to safeguard its sanctity and nurture its power, in private they are the perfect picture returning daily to the secret fountain of public power. The modern world stands in naked contempt of the contemporary "masters of media," drunk on the cheap bathtub gin of ratings and record sales.

Having tasted the new wine of the kingdom we must now go on imbibing, not in showmanship but in discipleship. Cultivating the habits of prayer and Bible study, joining and attending a Spirit-filled church and humbly seeking the Spirit daily are our means of staying drunk.

Having "received" the Holy Spirit, we now spend our lives, receiving the Spirit. That is no paradox. It is just the hair of the dog!

The Balanced Spirit-Filled Life

The Dual Antenna

❖

MINISTRY IN THE SPIRIT

*T*he masses attempted to formalize into words the difference between Jesus' preaching and that of the religious leaders of the day. "Because he taught as one who had authority, and not as their teachers of the law" (Matt. 7:29).

Notice that, though his miracles had certainly not gone unnoticed, the distinctive quality to which the people felt drawn was *authority*. Their world, not unlike our own, found its traditional societal underpinnings profoundly shaken. The pillars of government, culture and language had been very nearly swept away in the torrent of Greco-Roman world domination. In addition, the religious leadership of the day had degenerated into a compromised, powerless clique. The maddening public formalism, absorption with the law and political infighting combined with a sparsely camouflaged moral corruption had very nearly destroyed that leadership's credibility.

The ministry of Jesus of Nazareth must be viewed in contrast to the religious vacuum of his day. He ministered in a widening "confidence gap" between a confused, hungry populace and a backslidden, bound-up, ineffective, effete "clergy." Sound familiar?

We are facing an era of unprecedented disdain for its own clergy among America's laity. In a recent poll Americans confessed less confidence only in car salesmen and politicians than in the clergy. A long, simmering mistrust of seminaries by many in the mainline denominations is now finding open and angry expression. The booming phenomenon of "independent" churches is perhaps symptomatic of the disregard for clergy.·

The prevailing and frequently articulated opinion in such circles seems to be, "A Spirit-filled layman fully devoted to Christ, educated at the University of the Burning Bush and ready to believe God for miracles is more capable in real ministry than the seminary-trained, faithless, impotent denominational politicians being foisted off on many hapless local churches." At issue here is not the contemporary interpretation of the importance of ordination *or* of its definition. The point is that a laity, beset with a flood-tide of societal sins and personal problems, has no patience with a clergy incapacitated by form and denying the power of the supernatural. Liturgical experimentation only adds insult to injury.

The man whose teenagers are on dope and whose marriage is being destroyed by infidelity and despair holds in naked scorn attempts to comfort him by adding terpsichorean interpretations of the Lord's Prayer to the Sunday morning service. When one is clinging to soul and sanity with broken fingernails and shattered nerves, a service featuring a young lass leaping down the aisle in purple leotards and a sermon on Central American politics offer scant hope. Glitzy TV showmen with formulas for success, chanting mantras to own Cadillacs, pour salt in the wound.

The Key to Ministry

A recent article in a Methodist publication declared that "We

must redefine ministry to meet the needs of the nuclear age."
Hardly! We do *not* need to redefine ministry. We need to re-enter
it. The biblical ministry of healing, deliverance and authoritative proclamation of the gospel of full redemption goes undone
while whole denominations flounder in the "slough of despond."
Ragged armies of tired laymen look on in disgust as their cler-
gymen dissipate their calling on the utter irrelevancies of liberation theology, "inclusive language" and the election of bishops.

On the other hand many have been hardened in their skep-
ticism by the disastrous chicanery of some "televangelists." The
image-mongers and cynical manipulators have done much to
corrupt the *reality* of the ministry of the supernatural. The weak-
sister, suburban pastor without anointing has eroded its authority. A vicious one-two punch indeed!

The reason "the common people heard Jesus gladly" was because Jesus *ministered to their needs*. Leaving political protests
against Roman oppression to the Pharisees, Jesus cast out the
personal demons that held men and women in spiritual bondage.
Abandoning futile formalism to the priests, he cried out, "If anyone thirsts let him come to me!" Meanwhile he refused to hurl
himself from the pinnacle of the Temple in a spectacle that would
have ensured a huge ministry overnight. The people found in
Jesus' ministry the two elements conspicuously absent in the tas-
seled robes and flowery public prayers of the Pharisees: *reality*
and *authority*.

By reality I mean that Jesus' ministry was genuinely efficacious in people's lives. It was substance *not* image. When Jesus
spoke, people were *changed*. Some were healed. Others were
set free. Still more, like Zaccheus, were saved, sanctified and
called into responsible living. The presence, words and works
of the Nazarene wrought enduring and meaningful good in individuals. Far from the puny preachments of the Pharisees which
only condemned, Jesus actually set them free to "Go, and sin no
more" (John 8:11, KJV). He did not so much lecture on the
Mosaic law, he *sanctified* believers! In his sermon at Cornelius'
house (Acts 10) Peter was confronted with the prospect of try-

ing to explain the life and ministry of Jesus Christ to pagan Romans. How would he express to Gentiles, immersed in heathen polytheism, the ministry of the Jewish Messiah? Appealing to the Law and the prophets was useless. Peter must have been marvelously guided by the Holy Spirit. His words were sublime in their simplicity and exquisite in their effect. ". . . God anointed Jesus of Nazareth with the Holy Spirit and power, and how he went around doing good . . ." (Acts 10:38).

Unless Peter's words had been received with unyieldingly literal ears, however, they would have been wasted. The notion that amidst all his evil, a sinful man might occasionally "do good," is no novelty. Even Caesar may have occasionally been generous, gentle or truthful. The idea here is that Jesus did *always, only* good.

That must have been amazing to a Roman already longing to rise above the reprehensible evil of his day. Moreover, what a significant statement of the connection between nature and action. The point is that Jesus *did* good because he *was* good. Clearly the source of that "goodness" (Can we say holiness?) was also the power of his ministry, the Finger of God.

"How God anointed Jesus of Nazareth with the Holy Spirit and power, and how he went around doing good and healing all who were under the devil, because God was with Him" (Acts 10:38).

In Luke 11, Jesus claimed the Holy Spirit, the Finger of God, as the power source of His ministry of healing and deliverance. In Acts 10:38 Peter describes Jesus' ministry of "good" as being due to the Holy Spirit. In other words, Jesus, filled with the Spirit of wholeness, became a fountain of wholeness. Thoroughly good, he shed goodness where he walked. Healing and deliverance were not just "things Jesus did." They were the outward manifestations of an inward reality—holiness.

When the woman with the abnormal bleeding touched the hem of Jesus' garment she was instantly healed (Luke 8). Jesus demanded, "Who touched me?" Peter reminded the Lord that in the crowded streets perhaps dozens had touched him in only a few minutes. Jesus was speaking of far more than accidental contact. Someone had intentionally, deliberately tapped the fountain of *who Jesus was*. The power of holiness was virtue which could make the woman whole. That which flowed out of Jesus healed that which flowed out of her. She had touched the very core of his goodness. The goodness of Jesus and the goodness of his ministry are inseparable. Jesus said, "I do only what my Father tells me." In being totally sensitive and obedient to the Spirit of his Father, Jesus found the key to ministry. Yielded utterly to the will of God (What is that but sanctification?), he ministered in God's power wherever he walked.

Being Good, Doing Good

Man is not a sinner because he sins, and God is not holy just because he doesn't. Man sins because he *is* a sinner, and God does not sin because he *is* holy. The man Jesus, filled with the Spirit of holiness, *did* good because he *was* good.

That is the key to ministry in the Spirit. Partaking of God's *nature,* the minister "does" God's goodness. This is not arrogance. It is simply a statement of faith that human believers, sanctified by the very breath of goodness, incontestably can and will minister good in the power of the Finger of God.

Now by ministry I do not include only the ordained clergy. Every believer is in ministry. Teaching, counseling, interceding, testifying and soul-winning are not the work of the clergy alone. They are the purpose of God through all his children. Do not dare to say, "I have no ministry!" You have a ministry because you are a believer!

Wherever the Church is willing to lay aside exalted ambitions for glorious "ministries" and re-enter *the* ministry of being obedient to the Holy Spirit in the moment, unlimited power is immediately released. True Holy Spirit power for ministry flows out when faithful servants of God act in humility before his will. The Spirit-filled Church should fully expect the Spirit to flow out in healing, saving, redeeming, miraculous power.

Jesus said of John the Baptist, "No man born of woman is greater than he." Then, remarkably, he added, "Yet he that is least in the kingdom of God is greater than he."

The commentaries seem to enjoy a unanimity on this verse. They agree that Jesus is speaking of the "greatness" positionally of the least sinner redeemed by Calvary as compared to even the greatest prophet who lived before Calvary. Perhaps. Comparisons among his children were not usually the Lord's style.

What, however, if the Lord was speaking of someone specific? That changes the meaning considerably! "*He* that is least in the kingdom of God . . ." Who is *he*? Who is he that is least in his own control? Who is most humble before the sovereignty of God? Who is most willing to be the least of the least?

It is Jesus himself! There was never a man greater than he. I believe Jesus was speaking of himself. He "thought it not robbery to be equal with God," yet there was never a man including John himself, who found greater greatness in any greater humility. Andrew Murray called humility "the pearl of holiness." It is also the path of ministry.

Sensitive in Two Directions

God never had to break through the wall of Jesus' long range plans in order to call him into immediate action. There was no barrier of prejudicial pride that prevented his ministering to a lonely Samaritan women. No shell of egotism made him unable to love the leprous. Caution for his reputation never kept him from showing mercy to a woman taken in adultery. No man ever lived less bound by lust for greatness; no man ever ministered in greater power. The key to Jesus' whole ministry was in this. Resisting the claims of his own flesh and denying the passion for a great ministry he opened himself without reluctance to the power of God's Spirit. Apart from a willingness to be of no reputation we can hardly know true sensitivity to the Spirit. Ambition, pride and self-consciousness insulate us from the voice of the Spirit. It is easy perhaps for a man in Jimmy Swaggart's shoes to simply lose sight of his little private sins. They do not seem very important in the light of the cheering thousands. An arrogant sense of independence can stealthily creep in on the coattails of success. This is not to cast stones at Jimmy Swaggart. It is rather a reminder that fame and fortune can cloud true ministry even when the organization of a "ministry" is running at fever pitch.

If one word typifies Jesus' ministry it is *sensitivity*. Sensitivity is not only the fruit of humility, it is the essence of ministry in the Spirit. Jesus was able to hear at once with perfect clarity the voice of the Spirit and the voices of those to whom he ministered. He was able, free of himself, to let the Holy Spirit make sense of the unintelligible inner groanings of those about him.

For a modern analogy of ministry in the Spirit, visualize a satellite. It is in orbit between a distant space station and Earth. Via two antennae it receives simultaneous transmissions from both. These messages, one from Earth the other from the remote station, are fed into the on-board computer. There they are integrated and interpreted, and a response is formulated.

Likewise, ministry in the Spirit implies a two-fold sensitivity. The minister must be constantly, prayerfully, submissively sensitive to the impulses of the Holy Spirit *and* to the hurting humanity around him. Jesus said, "I do nothing of myself." In other words, "I never act independently. I hear my Father and I execute the sovereign mind."

Yet in the teeming streets of Jerusalem he was also instantly aware of the timid touch of one wounded woman. "Somebody touched me," he said.

If we lose contact with God, our ministry will be ruled by the flesh. We may substitute our own glorified ego or we may be cowed by others, but somehow the true supernatural power of the kingdom will be eroded.

Listening to God and People

One pastor told me he had asked his people to tell him what
to preach on. Absurd! First of all people don't know what they
need to hear. Second, if they knew, they would not tell him. Does
he seriously expect the man who is having an affair to request a
sermon on adultery? Woe to the preacher who hears only from
people! He or she quickly degenerates into a powerless replica
owned by the opinions of the congregation and not the power of
God.

The people will not hear from God unless the preacher has
heard from God. If the preacher is only hearing from the people
and his own flesh, his ministry will soon reflect only their corporate neurosis.

By the same token, we must not yield to any kind of mystic,
other-worldliness that comprehends ministry in a spiritual
vacuum. That was the failure of medieval monasticism. If we
wall ourselves in with God we may well wall out all possibility
of ministry.

We must train ourselves to really hear, to listen to others
around us. We must pray for sensitivity to the wounds and needs
of real folks. One of the great problems in seminaries today is
that much of the teaching is done by useless theoreticians and
political ax-grinders who have lost touch with where real people
actually live.

This is the challenge of ministry in the Spirit in counseling,
preaching or any other theater. Sensitive to the Holy Spirit and
broken to his own will, the minister is free to hear the "need" of
a congregation in a moment (not to deny the myriad individual
needs present) and the thrust of the Holy Spirit to address it.
Preaching in the Spirit is not so much the art of being fiery. It is
being yielded enough to preach in the stream of the Spirit in *that*
moment. This obviously requires hearing the need *and* obeying
it.

Preaching is ministry and preaching in the Spirit is
miraculous communication that defies all the laws of oratory.

Certainly I do not completely understand what anointing is. I know when it is there and when it is not! I believe that, at least in part, it is simply saying from the pulpit what the Holy Spirit is saying in the hearts of the listeners. When the outward voice of the preacher and the inward voice of the presence agree, the miracle of the preached Word is manifested.

Scripture says, "The Spirit and the bride say, 'Come!' And let him who hears say 'Come.' Whoever is thirsty, let him come ... (Rev. 22:17). This verse near the end of the New Testament speaks of that marvelous agreement between the voice of the bride and the voice of the Spirit. I am persuaded that is _exactly_ the mystery of anointing in preaching. When we proclaim to thirsty souls and the Spirit himself bears witness, the miracle of preached Word, the transcendent art of heaven, happens.

Years ago I was invited to preach the morning service at a small church near Athens, Georgia. I felt prepared, and I was eager to preach a certain message with a strong evangelistic appeal. Yet the nearer I got to that church the more uncomfortable I became with that message. I became aware of an inner stirring to teach on forgiveness. It is with shame I confess I denied that voice. I wanted to defend my reputation as an evangelist, and I did. I am sure that many present that morning would testify that the sermon was certainly lively and even yielded some response to the altar call.

In my heart, however, I knew something was wrong. The sermon was discordant and unsatisfying. Worse yet was what happened at the close of the service. The last person to leave the sanctuary that morning was a frail, pinched woman with a particularly joyless countenance.

After she left the pastor asked, "Do you know who that woman is?"

"No," I said.

"Six months ago," he explained, "her daughter was cruelly raped and beaten to death by two men. I believe she is dying of unforgiveness. How I have prayed for God to get through to her!"

In such a devastating moment nothing except broken-hearted repentance will do. I sat in my car and wept bitterly, asking God to help me in the future. (He has many times.) That morning however, I totally missed ministry in the Spirit for the sake of my own willful desire to preach a great "evangelistic" message. I preached one sermon while the Spirit was ready to *agree* with another. Until a preacher is crucified to his own sermon, he cannot be counted on to consistently, faithfully declare the whole counsel of God in the power of the Holy Spirit.

These two, *sensitivity* and *obedience*, are crucial in preaching and are indispensable in the exercise of the gifts of the Spirit. I applaud all sincere efforts to study these gifts and some excellent books have been written on that subject. A chapter more specifically related to gifts follows this one. Yet I believe there is something in the Holy Spirit that stubbornly resists categorization. The Finger of God simply will not make analysis and dissection easy.

The Need for Humility

Ministry in the gifts is less of methods and procedures and more of running before the wind. I know that certain gifts seem to find a residential quality in certain believers. Much hurt, however, has come to the body through talk of "having" the gifts. For example, to say that a believer *has* the gift of word of knowledge lends an inappropriate proprietary note to the matter.

I believe the gifts are *in* the Holy Spirit and in the believer only by virtue of his presence within. Power in preaching comes by being sensitive to what the Holy Spirit wants to be said to a specific congregation in a given service. The preacher must then flow into that channel. That message must necessarily be filtered through the experience, temperament and constitution of the preacher. Still the preacher dare not expect to be caught up in an ecstatic, out-of-body experience every time he preaches. It is often work. Strenuous, prayerful, diligent study and preparation do not inhibit the Spirit. They prepare the preacher.

By the same token, the other gifts as well are best demonstrated in a yielded, sanctified human vessel more sensitive to the Spirit himself than to his gifts. Humility is the key. If we are talented, educated, and clever enough to "handle it" we may be tempted to think we do not need the gifts. We must remember that all our knowledge of counseling methods is still only so much wood, hay and stubble unless God is there. How many precious opportunities in counseling have been squandered by counselors not in tune with what the Spirit was ready to reveal in that moment? How tragic, for example, are the poor, wounded creatures who sincerely seek help from the Church and come face-to-face with some Johnny-one-note who begins casting out demons when a more sensitive heart might hear the Lord's leading. The self-styled "specialist" who claims to *have* a ministry of deliverance may often be totally insensitive to the very Finger of God by which he hopes to minister deliverance. An immature charismatic casting demons out of the chairs and the smug psychologist who totally denies the supernatural have one thing in common. Both do minister in presumptuous arrogance denying their second-to-second need of God's Spirit.

A Fruity Scenario

A woman is praying softly while washing dishes in her home. She senses a sudden urge to make a fruitcake, take it next door and tell her neighbor of God's love. In obedience she acts quickly but with doubts. She rings her neighbor's bell, hands over the cake and says, "I just wanted you to know, God really loves you, and I wanted you to know that I'm here and I care."

To her shock her neighbor falls in her arms weeping and confesses a great need for God. In only a few moments of prayer the neighbor is gloriously saved!

The woman is overjoyed. Finally she knows what her "ministry" is! She calls a lawyer, raises some money and launches—

Fruit Cake Ministries, Inc.

The next day the Holy Spirit tries to urge the woman to call her pastor's wife with a word of encouragement. The woman cannot hear. She has no time. She has a board of directors meeting for Fruit Cake Ministries.

How many times we miss opportunities for genuine ministry in the Spirit because we are striving to develop our own little fruit cake corner of the kingdom! I flinch at the thought. My constant prayer is for sensitivity and my greatest daily battle is to fight back the strident demands of my "ministry," that I might hear when the Spirit calls me into his ministry.

The key to Jesus' magnificent ministry was that he resisted every urge to specialize and frustrated every effort of others to pigeon-hole him. Sensitive to the Spirit in every moment, Jesus heralded only what he heard, taught exactly as he was told and delivered only when he was directed.

How Jesus Did It

The perfect example is the Master's ministry with the Samaritan woman at the well (John 4:16-26). This was not some formula approach to cross-cultural evangelism. Far from it. Jesus was ministering in second-to-second, sentence-to-sentence dependence on the Spirit. By being least in his own power, he found the sheer greatness of ministry in the Spirit.

"Go, call your husband and come back," Jesus said (John 4:16).

Why, at that exact moment, did he say that? Did Jesus know what lay ahead in the conversation? It is more important, however, that he was simply following the momentary leading of the Spirit. To remember Jesus' humanity in no way denies his divinity. He was God to be sure. Yet he was God become *man*. He was proof that the mind of a real man can be informed by the mind of God.

The woman answered and said, "I have no husband."

Was she saying exactly what Jesus knew she would say? The point is that "ministry in the Spirit" in counseling, for example, demands following the Spirit up some avenues when we do not see the purpose. I think it is more likely that Jesus, supremely sensitive to the Spirit, yielded to the urging to call for her husband. At that point Jesus may not have known exactly where it was all leading. *He was sensitive to the Spirit at that point.*

When she answered, "I have no husband," Jesus' sensitivity was more to her. In her he discerned such a jumble of male spirits that he knew her sexual contacts had been multiple. Remember that in sex is spiritual communication, as well as physical. (There is something of this in 1 Cor. 6:16). As Jesus "listened" intently to what he "heard" in the woman, the Holy Spirit brought that discernment of Spirits into focus. Jesus now "saw" former husbands and a common-law lover. *He was sensitive to the woman at that point.*

When he revealed this knowledge to the woman she knew that the Spirit was with him. She was not convinced by doctrine; she was touched by the *ministry of the Spirit.* What a majestic demonstration of the gifts. As a result of the manifestation of power in Jesus' ministry, she found confidence to seek sound doctrine.

"Our fathers worshiped on this mountain but you Jews claim that the place where we must worship is in Jerusalem," (v. 20) she said, implying a question of who was right.

Jesus' answer was filled with supernatural wisdom instead of parochial self-defense. Rather than trying to give her some Jewish apologetic for Temple worship, the Master turned her thoughts to the character of God and the nature of true worship.

In that brief encounter Jesus perfectly demonstrated the power of sensitivity. Ministry in the Spirit, like the satellite with two antennae, implies receiving signals from two transmitters at the same time. We must learn to "tune in," to truly *hear* the spirit of those to whom we minister. At the same time we must learn to "hear with the other ear" the Spirit of God.

Look again at Jesus' ministry in the Spirit with the woman

at the well (John 4:10). Through his two-fold sensitivity to the woman *and* to the Spirit, he operated in the gifts of discernment of spirits, word of knowledge and word of wisdom. None of it was forced or awkward. The three gifts flowed together because of his *sensitivity* and *obedience.*

Examples From My Experience

Though we never flow in the gifts as fluently as Jesus did, I am persuaded that we minister in the same Spirit with the same gifts, as we learn sensitivity. Let me offer these examples.

At a revival in a tiny country church in Georgia I knelt to pray with a middle-aged woman in the altar. Her brown hair was pulled back severely from her face, only emphasizing her peculiarly expressionless countenance. At her side knelt a thin little girl who peeped curiously over the altar at her mother and me. "This is my daughter," the woman said. "She has a great many allergies. Please pray for her."

I heard her words. They were certainly not complicated. Yet it seemed as if beneath her mousey, demure exterior I could "hear" a scream. Where did it come from? What was the agony that was so deep it did not even give her an honest frown?

At the same time I thought that perhaps I sensed the Holy Spirit speaking to me. Not even a phrase, just a single word bleeped across that inner screen. It was "adopted." Nothing more, just "adopted." I am always fearful of leaping out ahead of the Lord on fleshly impulse, but the word seemed to grow stronger as I questioned her about the girl's physical afflictions.

Finally, I asked, "May I share with you what I seem to hear in my heart? I can miss the Lord as easily as the next person, but I feel right now that the Lord is speaking to me about adoption."

(This is a tack I have frequently taken in ministering in this theater. It seems to a more useful posture, perhaps less threatening to seekers than some of the authoritative pronouncements I have heard.)

"Let me ask you," I continued, "is she adopted?"

"No," the woman replied, "she's not."

I was caught off guard. I was so sure that she would say "yes" that I did not know where to go next.

"Are *you*, perhaps, adopted?" I asked, grasping for a straw.

"No," she answered flatly.

I was just about to drop it and move on when the little girl said, "Momma, Johnny is adopted."

Irritation flashed in the woman's eyes and her voice was laced with anger as she turned quickly to the girl. "I know!" she said sharply. "Don't you think—" As her eyes met mine again the words trailed off. The woman dropped her eyes and began pathetically wringing her hands. The mother, not the daughter, looked like a sad little girl caught with her hand in the cookie jar.

"I know," she sighed. "I knew what it meant the first second you said 'adopted.'"

"It's all right," I tried to reassure her. "Surely God only brought it up because he loves you and wants to do some healing."

"I certainly need it," she moaned.

She began to pour out the pain of 13 years. Having adopted a child, she had regretted it almost immediately. Never feeling quite able to love the boy, she was wallowing in self-pity and aching with guilt. It had very nearly poisoned the entire household.

I do not know how much healing she was able to receive that night. I do know she was confronted by the Finger of God supernaturally in a setting uniquely designed to at least allow her to begin being healed. The pastor agreed to continue counseling.

More Examples

Preaching one night at the campus of the University of South

Alabama at Mobile, I finished my sermon and gave the invitation. Young people were already walking the aisles when I thought the Spirit was impressing me to minister in a certain way. It was unfamiliar territory to me, and I waited to see if the urging would diminish. Instead it gained in intensity, and I tried to obey the best I knew how.

Stepping to the microphone, I said, "I believe I hear the Lord saying there is a young girl here tonight who has recently been diagnosed as having anorexia. Come down here tonight, and let us pray for you."

There was no possible way that I could know that Dr. Faye Roberts, a prominent Mobile pediatrician, had only that afternoon forcefully confronted a teenaged girl with the frightening truth. Despite the girl's attempts to hide it and deny it for several years, she had anorexia nervosa. Dr. Roberts, also a Spirit-filled Christian, brought the teenager and her brother to the on-campus evangelistic services that very evening.

Dr. Roberts and the girl's mother coaxed her to the altar, where they told me the story. I had never before prayed with anyone for healing from anorexia. *Lord,* I prayed silently, *Grant me supernatural wisdom. Minister through me to this poor girl. Oh, Finger of God, set this girl free, in Jesus' name.*

At that point I felt strongly directed to pray that she might have a supernatural visitation, an actual touch of God's love. I prayed, laying on hands, that perfect love would cast out all fear. It seemed as though we were all suddenly being bathed in love.

At that very moment Acts 10:15, "Do not call anything impure that God has made clean," came very clearly into my mind. After I shared that verse with her, the Lord led us together into a scene that was remarkable.

We visualized her entering a room with a long dining table. As she entered Jesus took her hand and led her to the table. The table was laden with a bountiful feast, and I listened as she described the various foods she saw.

Seated at the table were the saints of the faith, Paul, James, John and many others. She was shocked as Simon Peter, a turkey leg in his hand, called out to her gaily, "Come and eat!"

When she hesitated, I sensed that I should speak a prophetic word in the name of the Lord. "My daughter, I love you. My love sanctifies you. Never again call anything that I have cleansed unclean, especially yourself."

At this point I sensed some break inside her, and I began to simply pray for her healing and deliverance. The whole thing took less than 15 minutes but, "He doeth all things well."

Over the years since that night I have heard the girl, her mother, and Dr. Roberts testify to God's immediate deliverance. They thank God that there has never been a recurrence. Dr. Roberts later told a congregation in Mobile that in all her years of practice she had never seen an anorexic so dramatically and instantly healed.

It was immediate, powerful, sweet and total. And it was done by the Finger of God. Was it deliverance? Discernment of spirits? Perhaps word of knowledge? Did word of wisdom play a part? Was word of prophecy employed? The answer is all of the above. All of this urges me toward the conclusion that the gifts operate more in the moment than in the person.

I am also beginning to see that when the Spirit is free to flow in a moment of ministry, and as we remain sensitive and obedient, the gifts are frequently like grapes in a cluster. The secret, I believe, is learning to "listen" in two directions at once. Sensitive to those around us *and* sensitive to the Holy Spirit, we become gifted channels for ministry.

The third example is simple, yet important. My own mother serves in my office as my personal secretary. She is not a pastor. She is not "trained" in some particular discipline of ministry. She is however what we are *all* called to be—Spirit-filled.

At a certain youth meeting she passed a college boy she had never seen before. Stopping short she lightly touched his arm and peered into his face.

"Is there something wrong?" he asked.

"I don't know," I heard her reply. "Are you being treated for diabetes?"

"Why, no," he answered. "I am not a diabetic."

"Promise me," my mother said intently, "that as soon as you get home you will go to a doctor and be tested. I truly sense the Spirit telling me that you are a serious diabetic."

"Okay," the boy laughed, "I promise. But I am sure I am not."

Later I asked her if she had some material reason to believe that he was in fact a diabetic. She assured me that he looked perfectly normal to her. She was a bit unnerved by the incident herself and felt a little foolish.

Some days later, however, the boy called to express his deepest gratitude. Tests had revealed that he was a serious diabetic. The doctor, absolutely shocked at the results, immediately prescribed the strongest treatment possible.

Now, as far as I know, she has never been used in that way since. It would be a mistake to conclude that she "has" the gift of word of knowledge or any other gift. That is just the point. She was simply yielded, sensitive to God's voice and sensitive to *that* young man in *that* moment.

Ministry in the Spirit need not await ordination. Believers are to be fountains of his healing virtue. In testimony, in prayer, in soul-winning, in word and in the gifts we are enjoined by Scripture to minister to the whole world in the power of the Finger of God. Pat formulas will not prevail. True ministry in the Spirit defies all our cozy classifications and neat little theories. This is not necessarily the "easy" path. Our age is possessed of a literal lust for a "party line." Ministering in the Spirit is infinitely more than "voting the straight charismatic ticket." It is living, breathing, flowing in the goodness of God's Spirit of love. That power will not ever be totally systematized.

Of course, there are dreadful misuses of the gifts, but we must not allow paranoia to freeze the gifts of the Holy Spirit out of ministry. I do not have to fight those whose various emphasis in the area of the gifts are different from mine. God forbid! Neither do I have to defend my theological reputation by petty quibbling over terms and techniques. The more I consider the awesome prospect of any earthen vessel being used as a channel of power by the very Spirit of God, the less patience I have with silly arguments about initial evidences, necessary signs *and* so-called charismatic excess. What the world aches for today is true New Testament power for ministry flowing through holy vessels.

Some who call themselves charismatics have become so obsessed with some particular gift or aspect of ministry that they are utterly missing the thrill of freeing the Spirit to move uniquely in each circumstance. Others in absolute terror of being *charismatic*, limit the holy one of Israel. This childishness is not only counterproductive, it is downright sinful.

"Where the Spirit of the Lord is, there is liberty" (2 Cor. 3:17).

Grant it, Lord Jesus!

CHAPTER X

Unfathomable Modern Conceit

❖

THE GIFTS OF THE SPIRIT

*T*ragically, the gifts of the Spirit are often viewed as rare eruptions of the supernatural, bursting at random through the comfortable uniformity of an earthbound church. Even when the scriptural validity of the gifts is not flatly denied, they are often seen as the capricious displays of divine power through unique (and eccentric) vessels. In this way they are relegated to the level of sightings of the Loch Ness monster. Hence politic evangelicals never actually deny the biblical authority of gifts. They rather condescendingly allow that in each generation an interesting primordial throwback or two will arise, like Brigadoon, and manifest some particular gift. I mean, there is, after all, a place for a Kathryn Kuhlman now and then.

Such a murderous kindness only serves to foster a pathetic ignorance of the very powers in which God intended the body of Christ to minister. It further exacerbates the prevailing fear, suspicion and division surrounding the gifts of the Spirit. The neglect of the cultivation of the gifts is only deemed possible through the unfathomable modern conceit which imagines that politics and post-graduate degrees obviate the power of the Holy Spirit.

It is tragic indeed for the gifts of the Spirit to lie fallow while ministries go wanting for power. The gifts should be seen as neither odd nor unusual. Nor are they for the spiritual iconoclasts alone. The church should flow in these empowerments naturally, or perhaps it is more sensible to say supernaturally. Consider the various natural gifts or talents of a basketball team. There must be a regular balanced demonstration of all those talents. Jump shots, for example, must be a regular part of its plan. The basketball team which expects a jump shot only rarely, and then only from its super star, will see a victory even less often than it sees a jump shot. Likewise the gifts of the Spirit should be explored, developed, sought, employed and expected by the church. The church is defined by the very Finger of God who defined and empowered the ministry of Jesus. Therefore, we also must meet the woman at the well in the supernatural ministry of power. We are not filled with any Spirit save that same Spirit of holiness who filled Jesus. The gifts in which he ministered *are* also ours. We either use, abuse or neglect them; but they *are* ours!

In an effort to better understand and employ the gifts we must avoid categorizing them too tidily. There is danger in thinking of anything regarding the Spirit as fitting too easily into pigeonholes. Yet there is *much* to be learned and much room for growth.

There are at least three different scriptural perspectives on the gifts.

Gifts as Offices of Ministries (Romans 12:3-8)

Here the gifts are seen in their result. "Ministries" or informal offices in and to the body of Christ gradually take shape as persons consistently demonstrate particular gifts effectively. As persons in the body gradually gain repute for faithfully executing the gift given to them, their giftedness becomes a dependable asset to the community of faith.

When financial needs arise those who have faithfully, responsibly and generously cultivated the gift of giving will be counted on (not exploited) to "get the ball rolling." What a needed ministry! The prophecy given by untried neophytes usually means little. Yet as the body begins to gain confidence in the ministry of prophecy through certain responsible, trusted individuals in their midst, their words carry more weight. Those who need restoration will more frequently (though *not* exclusively) be guided to those whose ministry of mercy has been proven.

So many church committees and work areas have floundered pathetically because of misplaced ministries. It is counterproductive and downright unscriptural to elect or select persons to perform ministries which are inconsistent with their gifts. The nomination committee views the ministries of the church as pre-established empty slots to be filled by "the best people we can find."

The scriptural view sees the ministries of the church as the natural outgrowths of the consistent, faithful exercise of the gifts under the authority of the Church. Hence ministries develop *only* as believers cultivate the gifts before the watchful eyes of the body. Instead of dreaming up new ministries and trying to staff them, the New Testament Church must cultivate mature, gifted believers and channel them.

Gifts as Gifted Persons (Eph. 4:8-14)

In this provocative passage, the gifts are seen as actually being the gifted persons themselves. God sends gifted men and women to the body as "gifts of the Spirit." In a church in Kentucky, a woman confided in me in conspiratorial chagrin that,

"Our preacher thinks he is God's gift to the church."

"Hallelujah!" I responded brightly. "He is!" I tried to explain to the dumfounded woman. "I'm glad he knows it!"

The Holy Spirit is constantly moving to direct the right people to the right place at the right time. They are his timely "gifts" to the church. It is a precious work of the Spirit to raise up a Billy Graham just when the world needs one. In the itinerate ministry in which I have served for many years now, nothing rewards me more than when someone says, "God has brought you to our church (community/fellowship/family/campus/whatever) at exactly the right time."

It seems to be the expression of Eph. 4:11, that the result of those in the second category is the development of those in the first category. As apostles, prophets, evangelists, pastors and teachers faithfully fulfill their several offices, persons will be perfected for the work of the ministries such as exhorting, giving, administration and mercy. Obviously, there are areas of overlap but the principle is valid.

Perhaps the point is too finely made, but I believe that there is an obviously downward vertical leadership-concept expressed. We have too often failed to "perfect the saints" within the congregations to do ministry in that more localized context because we have stubbornly refused to tap into the greater ministries of apostleship, prophet, evangelist and so forth in the broader theater of the body corporate. In most mainline denominations the evangelist, for example, is at best a square peg in a round hole. At worst, many denominations have assumed an adversarial posture with those they have licensed to do that very work.

Special Notes

1. These lists of "ministry" gifts are probably not *inclusive*. It appears to me that Paul (Eph. 4:11) was more nearly teaching on using obvious examples in all these passages. I think it is usu-

ally counterproductive to build cast-iron rules, squeezing some persons into slots where they do not fit and lopping off others altogether because the correct label won't seem to stick. There is a flow, a graceful overlap that truly demonstrates body unity and must not be squashed by dogmatists.

2. These are not *exclusive*. By beginning to perfect the saints which gravitate into certain ministries, we must not lose the imagination to welcome newcomers and changes. Furthermore, as ministries enlarge and grow (or lose their vitality or anointing) of necessity we must not cling to outdated works and modes. As long as God is in it, it is ministry. After that it is a fossil.

3. We cannot become *possessive*. In Ephesians 4:12, Paul speaks of "the works of service, so that the body of Christ may be built up." We know that when the direction of the ministry turns inward toward the minister, dry rot begins to set in. When the pastor's salary assumes importance over vision for edifying the body, he or she begins to minister death.

I once received a letter from a United Methodist district superintendent in Alabama telling why he did not want me to preach at a one-night meeting in his district. His angry letter was so self-centered and possessive that I marveled he could not see it. We must remember this is not *our* church. These are not *our* people. The ministries to which we have been called are not *ours* at all.

Gifts as Manifestations (1 Corinthians 12)

Here the gifts of the Spirit are taken to mean the manifested, supernatural empowerments of the Holy Spirit in the individual believer. Those gifts are absolutely independent of natural abilities, constitutional predisposition and maturity. Spirit-filled believers may experience any or all of the gifts at different times and certain highly mature, deeply spiritual believers may never execute certain gifts.

The gifts in this view are the manifested power of the Holy

Spirit for ministry in the moment. They are proof of God's desire
to use believers supernaturally to minister in power to others.
They are *not* badges of merit.

Hardly any area of functional theology incites more controversy than the gifts of the Spirit. The lust to normalize one's
own experience will eventually lead to either of two equal and
opposite errors. Some will fall prey to an arrogant, presumptuous, "more-gifted-than-thou" emphasis on whatever gift they
have experienced. True ministry in the gifts never creates a
smug, self-satisfied "tongues-cult" more interested in the shib-
boleths of charismania than in the loving demonstration of the
Spirit of Jesus. Neither is it a mature, responsible, balanced approach to categorically halt the exercise of the gifts, *any* of the
gifts.

Sometimes an unwholesome attitude about gifts permeates
a fellowship (or grips an individual believer) and makes these
supernatural gifts into some sort of game of charismatic poker.
One can almost see folks occasionally plunk down their "cards"
in repulsive arrogance.

"*I* have tongues and prophecy!"

"Ah, ha," counters another gleefully, "I will see your tongues
and prophecy and I raise you word of knowledge and interpretation of tongues!" I always think of the woman who fell into an
abandoned well while walking in the woods. She promised God
that if he would get her out she would become a soul-winner.
She was soon rescued, and she remembered her promise. There-
after she would regularly lead some unsuspecting friend out into
the woods and push him or her into the well.

We must not expect everyone else to experience God in the
same hole in which we did. Nor must we deny them their own
unique ministries, experiences and expressions.

While this is not a book about the gifts of the Spirit I do want
to make a few comments about each gift and add a few general
notes. This is not an exhaustive treatment of the gifts, but it has
been helpful to me to study the gifts (those listed in I Cor. 12:8-
10) in this way.

Inspirational Gifts of Revelation—Word of Knowledge, Word of Wisdom, Discernment of Spirits

Word of Knowledge—

As it implies this means a specific knowledge relevant for ministry of which we are made aware *only* by the Spirit. This does not imply intelligence and is exclusive of gained knowledge such as mathematics or some other discipline of study. A knowledgeable person may never be used in word of knowledge while an ignorant one may be marvelously gifted in this way, or vice versa.

As we learn to listen with more boldness to those inner nudges of the Spirit, this gift can develop and be tremendously helpful in ministry. The hard part is having the courage to act on such a word when it comes.

For example, in a revival service near Dalton, Georgia a young woman answered the invitation and came weeping bitterly to the altar. I had never seen her before. I suddenly experienced a sense that her name was Gena. I was also aware of God's deep love for her as a person. I felt extremely unsure of what to do.

Finally I just knelt beside her and said, "Gena, the Lord knows you and he loves you."

If she had said, "My name is not Gena," I was determined to just skate past it the best I could and get on with ministering to her in prayer. Instead she looked up amazed.

"How did you know my name?" she asked.

"I believe the Lord revealed it to me," I answered, "to convince you that he loves *you* personally."

"Oh, thank God!" she gasped. "Thank God! I am in such terrible sin I thought surely God had forgotten me."

She was gloriously saved and is a marvelous Christian to this day.

As another example, in a service in Brisbane, Australia an elderly woman came forward for healing. A younger woman stood at her elbow assisting her. Neither had said a word when

I sensed the Spirit filling my mind with clear images and unbidden thoughts.

I said, "I sense in my mind that God is showing me idols. I see pictures draped in flowers hanging on the wall. I also see women reading tarot cards and dabbling in witchcraft."

The younger woman looked shocked and began speaking to the older woman in a foreign language. Now *I* was shocked. I had assumed they were both Australians. The older lady began to weep as she answered in the same language. Finally the younger girl spoke to me in English.

"This is amazing," she said. "This is my mother. She is Romanian. She grew up in orthodox faith. Those are the icons and the pictures. The women doing witchcraft are her mother and her aunts. I never knew about this!"

We prayed to break any spiritual bondage or attack of Satan that entered her as a little girl watching such evil. As we came against the spirit of affliction which was now attacking 50 years later and thousands of miles away, she testified to a great sense of God's deliverance. I do not have a follow-up report, but the point is that her faith was deeply touched by such a clear word of knowledge.

I believe more Spirit-filled Christians might move in this area if they would trust the mind of Christ within them. Of course, mistakes will be made. If you are too fragile to make a mistake, you are not hearty enough for ministry in the gifts of the Spirit.

I have made many mistakes. Sometimes what I truly thought was a word of knowledge was not confirmed. In such cases, I drop it *immediately* and pray for the humility and grace to learn from the mistake. I have learned a great deal from such failures and I have *not* seen anyone seriously hurt. God knows our hearts.

Word of Wisdom—

Word of wisdom is not so much a specific revealed fact or knowledge, it is a revealed truth, the application of a truth or the expression of a truth in a supernatural way.

Jesus said with respect to the woman taken in adultery, "Let him who is without sin cast the first stone." It was the perfect, anointed application of the word of wisdom.

Many in teaching, preaching, witnessing or counseling have experienced this phenomenon and not known what to call it. When this gift takes over and begins to operate, the body (or individuals within the body) will be greatly blessed as the hidden often becomes revealed in immediate power. I offer a very simple example.

On a small prayer retreat once, a woman spoke rather angrily during a sharing time. She said, "I have just about lost faith in prayer. My prayers just seem to bounce off the ceiling."

Suddenly I heard myself answering, "If your prayers reach the ceiling they have gone to far. God is not on the roof. Know ye not the kingdom of God is within you? Stop praying up to a distant God. He knows your thoughts even as you form them."

The woman acted as if someone had thrown a basin of cold water on her. She stared straight into my face and her mouth literally dropped open.

"Why that's right, isn't it?!" she responded. "I have been trying to reach heaven. Thank God."

The woman was absolutely wide-eyed with wonder. Everyone in the room sensed that it was a truly wonderful breakthrough for her. Now admittedly that may not be a very remarkable example. It is my experience that a *a word of wisdom* generally comes that way. It is out said and done in a moment but with an almost immediate witness of the Spirit. Often it is a "small," not so flamboyant gift but marvelous in its execution.

Discernment of Spirits—

It is my perception of the body of Christ that this gift is perhaps among the most needed ones today. For that reason I have devoted the next chapter to some of its broader applications. I will just say here that *discernment* (and mature, responsible, application of the gift) is needed in every Christian life. It is, furthermore, a supernatural gift which is extremely potent in the ministry of leadership.

Discernment is not merely the ability to know when someone is demonized or by what spirit. This gift may also serve to discern the inherent spirit of a teaching, ministry or minister. Neither is it to be understood only in negative terms. It can be a tremendously affirming gift as truth and goodness are discerned.

In John 1:47 Jesus saw Nathaniel approaching and said, "Here is a true Israelite in whom there is nothing false."

That must have been an encouraging discernment for Jesus *and* Nathaniel.

In Acts 8:23 Peter said to Simon the magician, "You are full of bitterness and captive to sin."

At times this precious gift may aid a local fellowship in knowing how to receive other gifts, in particular tongues, interpretation and prophecy. Diligent prayer should be made for the Spirit to pour this gift into mature veterans who have deep wisdom. The pastor or trusted elders, aware of the deceitfulness of spirits, must be constantly on guard against confusion, rebellion, performance and error among others.

In one meeting where I preached, a woman interrupted my sermon with a message in "tongues." I told her, "Not now, Sister, you are out of order."

She refused to be silent, saying, "I have a message from the Lord."

"No you don't," I told her. "*I* have a message from the Lord. He would not interrupt the one he gave me to give you one." She stridently continued. Finally the ushers assisted her out. She was screaming in "tongues" every step of the way. It hardly took great discernment to see that she was off the beam, but the account serves to demonstrate the concept, especially in its relationship to leadership.

Gifts of Communication—Tongues, Interpretation, Prophecy

Various Kinds of Tongues—
This is only one of the gifts listed in which it cannot be demonstrably proven that Jesus himself ministered. This may mean nothing except that there was such perfect communication between Jesus and his Father that it was unnecessary. There is, of course, also the possibility that Jesus used the gift in private during his long times of prayer. There is no direct evidence but many pray thus and Paul did. Neither possibility is particularly important, however. *Tongues* seem to take three different manifestations in Scripture and experience.

1. *Public Tongues with Interpretation* (I Cor. 14:27): This will often be for praise or general edification of the body and should not be confused with prophecy. I have often felt that the "interpretations" given in meetings are really prophecies precipitated by tongues. Hence, the valid interpretation is often actually skipped over.

A public message in tongues must always be done in order, under authority, with interpretation and witness with the Spirit. There should never be more than *three* in any meeting. They may be long, short, beautiful or not so pretty to hear, but they will always agree with Scripture.

2. *Private prayer in tongues*: This may be a daily experience of tremendous blessing for those who enjoy this gift. Paul prayed in tongues (1 Cor. 14:14-15). In fact, it is obvious that his was precious to him (v. 18).

Many testify that this is useful in times when their intellect has exhausted its resources in prayer. Through this gift one can "pray on" without intellectual knowledge or proper vocabulary. In healing and praise it seems to be especially helpful.

3. *Tongues as a specific human language*: It seems apparent from Acts 2 that the gift of tongues manifested at Pentecost came as known languages which the disciples had never learned. Even today missionaries and others testify to examples of this

miraculous gift. I am not certain whether or not I have experienced this gift. The closest I have personally seen is recorded in my book *Launch Out Into The Deep* (p. 70, Bristol Books).

The incident occurred in Mexico many years ago, before I had learned any Spanish. One evening in a small village our interpreter did not show up for the meeting. None of the other five Americans present spoke any Spanish. Yet when I stood up to bring greetings, Spanish words and phrases sprang into my mind. I preached 30 minutes in a language I had never learned.

I was *not* speaking in tongues! I was thinking and speaking in Spanish. Perhaps what happened is that the Holy Spirit took all the Spanish I had heard from the simultaneous translations of sermons for the 10 day mission. Perhaps hearing 15 sermons translated gave me some kind of miraculous recall. I do not really know. I do know that whatever happened, it was a miracle of communication.

One note ought be made concerning the Acts 2 account. All my life it has been taught to me that those in the Upper Room were speaking not in unknown tongues but in a variety of earthly languages. The obvious rationale for this is Acts 2:7-11. Please notice however that *all* those listening seem to hear *all* those speaking in *his* own native language (Acts 2:8). Remember there were 120 speaking, presumably at once, to a crowd of at least 5,000! If the disciples were just preaching in the 13 or 14 languages listed how difficult it might have been for those listening to pick out their own languages. Yet there seems to have been a complete comprehension.

I suggest the possibility that a miraculous anointing may have been upon both speakers and hearers. From the text it appears to be possible that the 120 were praising God in "unknown" tongues and that God "short-circuited" the interpretation, allowing each listener to hear in his own language. I am not going to war over the point, but it seems highly possible, if not probable, to me. Be that as it may, however, the point is that tongues may take shape as a "specific language," being supernaturally communicated.

Special Notes on Tongues—

The idea that Paul's statement in 1 Cor. 14:18 meant that he was multi-lingual, as one Wesleyan pastor told me, is utterly unsupportable! If that is all Paul meant by verse 18, it is completely without meaning in the context.

Furthermore, I suppose I must mention the United Methodist Articles of Religion. One Methodist pastor pointed to Number *15*, which states (in paraphrase) that it is repugnant for public prayer to be in a language not understood by all.

"That," he argued, "precludes tongues in the United Methodist Church."

Ridiculous! That article has nothing whatsoever to do with unknown tongues. Wesley included that as a safeguard against the Roman Catholic use of Latin for the Mass ever becoming a Methodist practice.

There is no biblical passage which clearly teaches that tongues, or any other gift, is the necessary or initial evidence of baptism in the Spirit. Some may choose to emphasize such a teaching, but nothing of the sort is clear from Scripture.

I believe it may be true that many who do not now speak in tongues might be facilitated to receive this gift. The same could be said of *all* the gifts. The important thing is to create an atmosphere of loving acceptance, responsible participation and liberty with order. Such an ambience will be efficacious in helping believers be gifted, empowered and well-balanced. Attitudes of reactionary denial, infantile resistance and dogmatic insistances upon "evidence" will not prove helpful.

Interpretation of Tongues—

A clear distinction should be made between "interpretation of tongues" and translation of a language. In normal translation no spiritual endowment whatsoever is implied. A bilingual person simply transposes as carefully as possible, given his or her knowledge of the two languages. I have used translators all over the world. Certainly some are more facile than others; one might even say "gifted," but that is only in the way one might be "gifted" at the piano or in basketball. Once in Africa I was forced to use an Anglican priest with liquor on his breath as a translator.

The "interpretation of tongues," listed in 1 Corinthians 12, is something quite different. From my own experience and the accounts of others, the gift seems to be imprecise. As one person speaks aloud in tongues, another senses the Spirit giving insight into the meaning. Specific syllables, or sounds, will *not* suddenly take on exact meaning. *That* is translation. Instead, the idea or thrust of the message will begin to take shape.

My friend, Dr. Kenneth Kinghorn of Asbury Theological Seminary, feels that the public use of tongues will always be for praise. Hence, he says, interpretations should also be along the lines of praise. In Acts 2:11 those speaking in tongues spoke of the "wonders of God." Also in 1 Corinthians 14:2, Paul says, "For anyone who speaks in a tongue does not speak to men but to God."

Certainly these texts, especially I Corinthians 14:2, seem to back up Dr. Kinghorn's assertion. I am not prepared to be quite as categorical as he, but his point is important. Furthermore, I believe that many of the "interpretations" I have heard in meetings were not interpretations at all but prophetic utterances stimulated by an utterance in tongues.

It might, perhaps, often go something like this.

Speaker A: Tongues

Speaker B: A word of prophecy (not the interpretation!)

Speaker C: Remains silent, though frustrated, because the "interpretation" does not seem to "jive" with his spirit.

What then are some solutions? Some helpful possibilities are:

1. The pastor and/or, several very mature leaders should exercise discernment before accepting any gifts, especially tongues and interpretation. If the interpretation does not satisfy the "panel," they might lovingly say, "We feel the Spirit directing us to expect a different interpretation to that message. We will wait a moment more."

2. Some churches have only a few proven, mature and gifted people in this area who are set aside for interpretation. In churches where many visitors are common this may be important.

3. These two gifts may lend themselves more to smaller, intimate meetings, such as cell groups or house fellowships rather than large open services.

The point is that somehow order must be maintained, and responsible leadership must not yield to the injudicious and immature. There should be an atmosphere of unruffled, loving authority. When actually giving an interpretation aloud in a meeting these things should be kept in mind:

1. The person speaking should not expect the whole message at first. Perhaps only a brief sentence may be in mind to begin with. Give that. As more comes, share it.

2. Do not worry about the length. The interpretation may be much shorter than the tongues-speaking. Neither should it be too long. Here the leader must stay in loving control or spiritual "show-offs" will take over the meeting! Sad but it happens.

3. Do *not* use a false voice!

4. Do not be concerned if the grammar is incorrect and the vocabulary limited. God uses earthen vessels knowing their limitations. I have heard some interpretations that were not at all flowery and in the poorest of grammar yet they touched me *deeply*.

I would like to give one example of the exercise of this gift when I *knew* God was in it powerfully. I had a group of American students with me visiting Juan Wesley Seminario in Monterrey, Mexico. In a morning chapel service one of the Mexican boys gave a message in tongues. Wesley President Baltazar Gonzales gave the interpretation in Spanish. Then a bilingual student translated that into English. What might have been awkward and time-consuming became a moment of tremendous spiritual power. Almost every one of us wound up on the floor weeping, and a deep spirit of conviction and repentance fell on the group.

Word of Prophecy—

This can be a very powerful gift when exercised in the Spirit. I have seen this gift absolutely break a spiritual log-jam like dynamite. A prophecy may come in a predictable or nonpredictable form. It may simply be a public expression of what God wants said in a moment.

Such words *must* be clear, understandable, straight to the point and should be "accepted" by the body carefully.

The very day I received baptism in the Spirit I heard perhaps the most powerful, direct, anointed, specific word of prophecy so far in my life. We were a group of 150 United Methodist pastors assembled to study the Holy Spirit in December of 1975. One of the speakers at that conference, Dr. Ralph Wilkerson, said, "Someone here has a word of prophecy. Please give it now."

Rev. James Weldon was the one God used. I believe James was more surprised than anyone. When James stood and began to speak, the power of heaven was unleashed in the room.

"There is going to come a revival in North Georgia and it is beginning now."

When that prophecy came forth a phenomenal visitation of the Spirit of holiness filled the room. That prophecy has been and is being fulfilled, by the way, in some very specific ways.

At a Methodist church near Atlanta, Georgia, during a service where I was preaching the pastor gave a sober prophecy.

"I believe the Lord says that there is a man here who is being violent in his home. God is giving you this last chance to repent and confess or you will not see another year."

I was stunned at such a prophecy, but within a few weeks a man in the church died suddenly. It was only then that his wife had confirmed that he had been violent. That night they had been in the service and later they had discussed the pastor's prophecy, but he had hardened his heart.

Gifts of Demonstration—Miracles, Faith, Healing

These three gifts demonstrate very well what I mean by the gifts being rather like "clusters on the same vine." Though they may all be completely independent, it is difficult to imagine someone exercising the gift of miracles without also using the gift of faith. In much the same way, miracles are often, though not always, in the area of healing.

In Acts 3 the healing of the lame beggar is the perfect example. Somehow Peter *knew* a miracle was about to happen (faith). He spoke in authority and the man stood (miracle). The miracle was one of physical restoration (healing).

These three gifts usually have a far less residential quality than the others. They tend to appear in moments of need and are more apt than the others perhaps to be occasional rather than consistent in the life of the believer. They are more or less self-explanatory but some brief notes might be useful.

Healing and Miracles—

A miracle need not be one of healing, but in order to qualify it must be immediate, complete and in violation of the natural laws. Jesus turned water into wine. That was a miracle which had nothing to do with healing. Other examples would include walking on water and the multiplication of fish and bread. Not all healings are miracles. We may use the term loosely in reference to such wonders as childbirth or even the "miracle of flight," but they are not true miracles. Some healings are partial, progressive, aided by prayer and/or aided by medicine, but a miracle must be an instantaneous demonstration of God's power over nature.

The Greek term translated *miracle* might be better rendered "the focusing of power." In other words it is as if God suddenly focuses his power on one tiny spot in the universe and miraculously manifests his hand. That Greek term translated *healing* is seen to a clearer advantage if rendered "the graces of cures." These terms reveal the difference. Healing is a more diffused, subtle move of God. It is often slower or perhaps softer. It may imply mental, emotional, psychological and physical healing. Deliverance is included. A miracle is the immediate full result of a focusing of God's power. It is clearly a touch of the Finger of God.

We must be very careful about shouting "miracle" too quickly. A true miracle will announce itself without an advertising campaign. I do not know if there are such things as "big" miracles or "little" miracles. I suspect that the really impressive miracle is the one *we* need at the moment.

Faith—

The gift of faith must somehow be different from the "normal" faith operative in all believers. Certainly even faith for salvation is a gift in one sense, but this is something else altogether. This gift is an absolute, unquestioning "knowing" faith for something specific. This kind of faith need not be sought nor is it mustered and increased by will. It is a gift, given as any other gift. Suddenly one simply *knows*, absolutely knows, that God has spoken.

Once on my way to pray for a seriously sick brother I suddenly knew all was settled. I have seldom sensed anything quite like that. I knew he was going to be healed. It was almost as though he had already been healed. Upon arriving at his apartment another man and I laid hands on him and prayed. Under our hands his fever instantly broke. He immediately got out of bed, showered and dressed, and drove with us to the worship service at which he led the singing!

Certainly he was healed. Perhaps it even qualifies as miraculous though it was not very spectacular. The aspect of the event I shall always cherish, though, was that sudden, unexpected, absolute *faith* God dropped down into my spirit.

❖ ❖ ❖

The gifts of the Spirit are real. They are for the Church, and they are for today. None of them is to be universally expected and none is to be denied. They must be acted upon to be received. We can always dismiss and refuse a word of knowledge, for example, even as the Spirit may be attempting to grant one. We can simply *not* speak in tongues. All that is necessary is to just keep our mouths shut. The spirit of the prophet is subject to the prophet. All the gifts must be exercised in humility and submitted under authority. We are enjoined to seek the gifts in Scripture and we are forbidden to forbid them. They must never by toyed with nor blasphemed. Finally, they are not ours to hold, withhold or boast of. They are just as it says, gifts of the Spirit.

Come, Holy Spirit; show us how to be the best stewards possible of these supernatural gifts, that God may be glorified in us.

CHAPTER XI

Of Spiritual Nitwits

❖

MORE ON THE GIFTS

"*I* have a word from God," said the intense woman across from me. "The Lord has sent me here to give you a message."

She went on to inform me that the child of one of our Trinity Foundation missionaries was surely going to die and that God would hold me accountable. She was sincere, intensely sincere, and not deliberately trying to discourage and confuse me. Yet I had absolutely no witness at all that the woman "had a message from God."

There is a great new awakening in the church to the gifts of the Spirit. This is a blessing, of course. Paul did extensive teaching on the gifts, encouraged their orderly use, and confessed his gratitude for the frequency of tongues, for example, in his own life. Yet he was obviously aware from the start that it was an area in which problems would easily arise.

There have always been those like the foolish, feverish woman in my office who "prophesied" without delivering the goods. Several contemporary denominations have over-reacted to the difficulties presented by the gifts in ministry. It is amazing that otherwise evangelical and biblically sound believers blithely disregard Paul's command, ". . . do *not* forbid speaking in tongues" (1 Cor. 14:39). To do so is to blatantly disobey biblical authority, to quench the Spirit and to limit the Holy One of Israel.

We dare not allow ourselves to over-react to the kind of hyper-spiritual nitwits who make hair-brained and dangerous predictions in the name of God. Infantile bans on the gifts are a frank admission of a childish unwillingness to wrestle with thorny issues. They reveal the kind of paranoid imbalance that says, "Because a bull once gored a man, we will kill all bulls in all the world." Obviously, such voices would say, there was a time when God intended for bulls to exist, but in our advanced technological society bulls are simply too dangerous and not worth the risks. Perhaps some might even add, "The time for bulls died with the last mounted cowboys, and these lethal creatures now killing people in the streets are not real bulls at all but demonic imitations." How droll!

Maturity demands that we respond with balance, seeking safeguards, disciplines and checks which will allow us to minister in the gifts without cracking each other's skulls.

No Short-Cut to Maturity

Wisdom is gained by experience and growth. To slam the door on this area of the gifts because of its inherent difficulties is to say that public evangelism must be stopped because of the manipulation and money-grubbing of some evangelists. Shall we then cease all work among the poor and needy because of the errors, excesses and sins of the liberation theologians?

One passage from Scripture seems particularly helpful in expressing the mature balance so needful at this point!

Let this mind be in you, which was also in Christ

Jesus: Who, being in the form of God, thought it not robbery to be equal with God: But made Himself of no reputation, and took upon Him the form of a servant, and was made in the likeness of men: And being found in fashion as a man, He humbled Himself, and became obedient unto death, even the death of the cross. Wherefore God also hath highly exalted Him, and given him a name which is above every name: That at the name of Jesus every knee should bow, of things in heaven and things in earth, and things under the earth; And every tongue should confess that Jesus Christ is Lord to the glory of God the Father (Phil. 2:5-11, KJV).

The secret of the majestic way in which God glorified himself in the life of Jesus is humility. Note the words . . . "made himself nothing" (of no reputation). If Jesus had simply been seeking a reputation he could have chosen a much easier path than the cross. The Lord's temptation on the Temple pinnacle was one of reputation. If Jesus had indeed cast himself down safely he would surely have been an overnight success! That could have been the beginning of a ministry that reached the whole world, without a hint of the pain at Calvary. It was with *this* possibility that Satan tempted Jesus.

I believe that the temptation to clutch at a reputation for spirituality is at the heart of many errors in the exercise of the gifts. There is simply no short-cut to maturity. Upon hearing Jascha Heifetz play a violin concerto a woman said to him, "I would give my life to play the way you do!"

"*I* did, Madame," the musician answered. "I did."

Learning to hear God is a life's work. There will be failures, barriers, successes, joys and disappointments in the learning. It is definitely not a work to be attempted by sissies and get-rich-quickers.

As Opening to Satan

I once preached in a charismatic church that was on the verge of splitting. (It finally did!) One had the sense the whole time that there was an undercurrent of tension and suspicion. Finally I was asked to sit in on a meeting of the board of elders and the pastors. It was a disaster. I was no help to them, and they discouraged me.

One man seemed to be at the vortex of the conflict. I began to see in him anger and pride very near the surface of his emotions. Yet it was he who claimed to represent those who wanted the church to be more "spiritual."

"What we want," he said through gritted teeth," is for the pastor to take the lid off the gifts in this church. He wants everything submitted to *him*! There are some of us in this church who want the Holy Spirit to get free. That is all we want."

"No, sir," I responded in boldness born of being a visitor (one of the luxuries of being a guest preacher), "I do not believe that is all you want. I believe you want to be the pastor. This man has paid the dues; you want to ride in on the 'gifts express'."

"That is not true!" he said vehemently. "I do *not* want to be the pastor. I am a college professor. But I will not let this pastor run off those who want to use the gifts."

For all his denials, however, the college professor managed to get rid of the pastor only a few months later. Guess who became the new pastor! The "Spirit-filled" college professor, of course. By manipulation and Machiavellian politics the professor pulled a coup d'état and called it the work of God. You will know them by their fruits not their gifts.

How can the gifts flow in an atmosphere of willful disobedient, unsubmitted, prideful, selfish, arrogance? That is what I felt in that elders' meeting, and it is opening the door to Satan among many who sincerely want to see the supernatural gifts at work but do not have the "mind of Christ."

"The mind of Christ" is the synapse between the fruits and the gifts. Such a phrase as "the mind of Christ" immediately speaks of the gifts, especially those of word of knowledge, word of wisdom and discernment of spirits. Obviously they are mind-oriented or thought-oriented gifts.

By claiming the reality of Philippians 2:5, these gifts assume fresh credulity indeed. They might be seen as Jesus "accessing the computer bank of the human brain." Hence a word of knowledge, for example, comes as a thought. The challenge is in gaining the maturity and experience to sort out the thoughts Christ is thinking through us from random bursts of electricity and impulses of the flesh.

In addition to a deep knowledge of Scripture, the best—perhaps only and certainly most obvious—way to do this is to be in tune with the character, nature and style of Christ. The closer we are to him the more apt we are to hear his softest whisper above the strident shouts of other voices. Certain thoughts can be disregarded immediately if they are patently inconsistent with all we have found the Master to be in our own lives. The gifts will not manifest themselves through us in ways that contradict the character of Christ.

Words of knowledge which are showy, drawing attention to the individual and which are insensitive and hurtful are not from God. It is unlikely that God will give a preacher the ability to read the numerals on a 50 dollar bill in someone's wallet to convince him to put it in the offering plate. Not every word of knowledge, or any other "gift," is of God. Neither is accuracy, per se, a sufficient test.

In Acts 16:17, a young girl accurately identified Paul and his entourage as "servants of the Most High God" who would show others "the way to be saved." On the surface she was right on target. A less discerning evangelist than Paul himself might, in fact, have enjoyed the free publicity.

Paul, however, saw the disturbing, disorderly manner in which the girl repeated the phrase day after day. She flitted about the edge of his meetings, calling out her "truth" at inappropriate moments. Furthermore, at times she used the same gift to garner gain for her owners and renown for herself. Far from making herself of no reputation, she was making a spectacle of her "gifts." She needed deliverance, not election to the board of deacons. Even though what she said was "true" she did not have the true mind of Christ.

The angry elder of a charismatic church who uses manipulation, politics and subtle gossip to subvert the pastor is so obviously outside the mind of Christ that he ought to be rebuked and disciplined, not tapped for leadership. He needs deliverance, not deaconship. He has not made himself of no reputation, nor taken the form of a servant, nor become obedient. He has clutched at reputation, usurped authority and revealed his rebellion.

On the other hand those who deny the reality of the gifts have underestimated what it means to have "the mind of Christ." 1 Corinthians 2:16 asks, "'For who has known the mind of the Lord that he may instruct him?' But we have the mind of Christ."

J. B. Phillips in his Bible translation marvelously renders the last part of that verse, "We who are spiritual will think the thoughts of Jesus." Hallelujah! Those who are truly spiritual, and not just charismatic windbags, can expect to share in Jesus' thoughts. The more in touch with love, sensitivity, holiness, gentleness, meekness and the humility of Christ a believer is, the more he or she may share in the true gifts to God's glory.

Thinking Like Jesus

When the Finger of God writes *HOLY TO THE LORD* in the flesh of a heart, the Spirit of Jesus, the very mind of Christ, begins to replace the mind of Adam. That same mind of Christ begins to dilate the puny brain of the believer to "think the thoughts of Jesus."

The more we yield to Jesus' will, the more we think *like Jesus*. The more we think *like Jesus*, the more he thinks *in us*. In Luke 11, Jesus asks "Which of you fathers, if your son asks for a fish, will give him a snake instead?"

The obvious parallel is to the fatherhood of God. As we draw near with faith, believing the Holy Spirit to fill us, God will not give us mean-spirited, shallow, hurtful, confusing thoughts. We shall share in the thoughts of Jesus to whom the secrets of all hearts are disclosed. Call it word of knowledge, or wisdom or discernment of spirits; what it comes down to, is the *thoughts of Jesus.*

It is impossible to think thoughts that are not in your mind. But if Jesus' mind is in yours, you may well think his. By the same token, however, we must seek the true mind of Christ and not any other. If we want his thoughts, we must seek his servanthood. If we would have his guidance, we must long for his godliness. If we want his "knowing," we must know no reputation.

There is a possibly apocryphal story which illustrates this truth. Throughout the years of bloody conflict in the American civil war, one general made a consistent, unwavering witness of Christ to his troops and his superiors alike. His own commanding general, Sherman, had often made light of such faith.

Finally with the war ended, Sherman called the general to his headquarters in Washington D.C. on the eve of the victory parade down Pennsylvania Avenue. The parade was to be the high point of many lives. The President himself would be there, as thousands cheered the triumphant armies of the North. General Sherman had sobering words indeed.

"My friend," he began, "I am going to ask you to stand aside tomorrow and allow an associate of mine to lead your troops in the parade."

"What?" gasped the startled man.

"Yes," Sherman continued, "He was with me at West Point. He faithfully served here in Washington during the entire war but he as no troops to lead tomorrow. He has officially asked me to give him your place. I *intend* to grant his request."

"But my general," the shocked officer replied, "This is unjust. I led those men in battle. I deserve this one moment of honor."

"That is true," Sherman answered. "But you have been telling me for four years that you are a *Christian*. If you *are* a Christian, then stand aside."

"All right," said the officer. "On that basis I will gladly stand aside. As an officer, I protest, but as a follower of Jesus, I will happily give up my place. Let him lead, I will ride with the enlisted men in the column."

"That's all I wanted to hear." said Sherman, with a lilt in his voice and a sudden twinkle in his eye. "Let him ride at the head of your column. You shall ride at my right hand at the head of the whole army!"

We do not have to put ourselves forward. When Christ made himself of no reputation, his Father God lifted him up above all others. When we yield up our reputations as a sacrifice, he accepts that and in the final moment he will vindicate his name as well as all those who have taken the mind of Christ. In Twi, a language of Ghana, they say, *"Onyame Beckyere,"* "God will provide in the end."

That is true if we will let him. When we grasp for power, jockey for position and claim a reputation for spirituality we totter on the brink of losing all. The one who presses angrily forward, demanding that his "prophecy" be heard, refusing to submit his "gifts" to authority has not the mind of Christ. The very thing—the thoughts of Jesus for others—that would propel him into the spotlight will soon be soiled and useless.

We must resist short-cuts, stop defending our reputations and commit our promotions into God's hands. When the Word became a man, even the servant of men, God through him demonstrated his great power for healing, miracles and gifts! Let him who would be the most gifted servant of God now become the most giving servant of humanity.

We need not worry that it will come to nothing. That temporal concern is swallowed up in eternity. We can clutch at fleeting moments of man-made glory *now* and call it ministry. Or we can rest in Jesus and believe that, as we make ourselves of no reputation, he will let us stand in his glory in that day. Better an eternity in the glory that streams from the throne of the Lamb than 30 years in the admiration of undiscerning men and women.

Onyame Beckyere!

CHAPTER XII

Forbidden Perfume

❖

WORSHIP IN THE SPIRIT

"*L*et us all stand and say the pledge of allegiance," said the handsome high school boy. The president of the student body was leading a brief opening ceremony at the assembly of a large high school where I was to speak.

The thousand or so students lumbered to their feet, some even listlessly placed their hands in the general proximity of their hearts and prepared to drone through the familiar incantation. Suddenly, however, as the words of their young, blond president boomed over the P.A., giggles began to spread through the auditorium like ripples.

Not realizing he was the cause of the indecorous snickering, the youthful politician gamely raised his voice, "Our Father which art in heaven, hallowed be thy name. . . ."

With no less ludicrous results, congregations, pastors and liturgists have often droned hollowly through unengaging Sunday formalities and dared to call it worship. Not unlike the lad who accidentally launched into the Lord's Prayer, they have become unconscious of the content and absolutely disconnected from the act as expressive of anything in their own lives. The student body president summoned his peers to repeat the pledge of allegiance because that is how all high school assemblies he had ever seen began. He was clearly not expressing his own patriotic devotion, nor was he effectively inviting anyone else's.

The oil of praise was made by God's formula. Dictated by the Word (Exodus 30:31) and written down by Moses, it was mixed by the sons of Aaron, from age to age the same.

All Israel knew it to have a sweeter smell than the most precious perfumes of the daughters of Egypt. But to use it for personal pleasure or, worse, for sensual attraction, was expressly forbidden. "Do not pour it on men's bodies" (Ex. 30:32).

Why was this restriction so important to God? The problem is people's lust to take worship, like everything else they behold, into their own hands. God abhors worship that is people-centered, people-directed, people-powered and from which people take subtle profit.

When, in the spirit of Cain, a person takes it upon himself or herself to substitute an illegal sacrifice (grain for blood), obedience and true worship yield to pride and self-service. Quite simply, Cain created worship to his own liking.

Modern Pagan Worship

Now an obvious and particularly noxious form of this is to be seen in excessively emotional displays of Pentecostal enthusiasm. They are an inexcusable embarrassment to the true spirit of Pentecost. Underline, however, the words *true* and *false*. What catastrophe befalls a people who fear excess to such an extent that they shut out the Holy Spirit who lends life and liberty to worship!

In an age of cold-blooded religious formality, over-caution about Pentecostal excess seems somewhat wasted. The flesh can more subtly, but no less thoroughly, crowd out true praise in those passionless parades of robes and rituals and candle-lighting which we call modern worship. When the choir is seeking ego gratification, the choir director wants to prove that she has been to Julliard, the congregation is personally prayerless and the preacher is more concerned with his stole than soul, how can there be worship?

Recently, a seminarian told me of a course he was taking called "Preaching as Performance." No wonder we have so little true praise! When the preaching is performance, the praise will surely be pretense.

It is nightmarish even to imagine how many "worship services" in America each Sunday morning are person-centered, fleshly exercises in cultural elitism that glorify the choir director, Beethoven or the pastor's jokes. The typical contemporary American churchgoers have only fleeting glimpses of true spiritual worship. Their usual Lord's day experience is more nearly a self-conscious stroll through *Vanity Fair*.

When posturing preachers lead bovine congregations in the dull-witted repetition of antiquated orders of "worship," it is not worship at all! True Christian worship is Spirit-led, Spirit-breathed, Christ-centered and glorifies only God.

In seminary I was actually taught that worship service is a performance. I was told that the congregation are the performers, the leaders are the prompters and God is the audience. That is the perfect picture of paganism. Pagans believe that the gods must be appeased or satisfied with worship. Hence, they contrive more and more elaborate "worship" replete with rituals, rites and costumes in order to entertain the audience of gods.

The Intimacy of Christian Worship

True Christian worship, however, exists without audiences just as surely as the intimate exchanges of lovers. In fact, that is exactly what Christian worship is; it is the exchange of love between the bride and the lover of her soul.

Standing in the Los Angeles International Airport I watched a young woman await and greet a sailor with unfeigned spontaneity. As the tall, gawky seaman ambled into the terminal, his girlfriend literally leapt around his neck, showering him with kisses. He twirled around in a circle lifting her completely off the ground. The simplicity and happiness of the moment was memorable.

That is also the essence of worship! When believers pour out their affection on God, does he remain aloof, untouched, implacably distant? Hardly. God is not a critical audience watching to see if we light the candles correctly. He is a participant seeking what we are seeking. God, no less than we, longs to enter into sweet communion.

The girl in the airport was not performing for the sailor or the bystanders. She was simply acting out of the reservoir of her love for him, and he responded in kind. When we lift our arms to our Father and sing, praise, pray and rejoice in his presence, he takes delight.

To worship is to enter into the presence of the Lord. It is *not* man-centered "performance." To use worship to glorify the choir or preacher is using the oil of the tabernacle to perfume the whore of Babylon. Worship is a divine encounter. Paganism hopes by ritual and pageantry to pacify its spectator-gods and appeal to human pride. Christian praise humbly, joyfully, thankfully enters into worship in the awesome expectation that God enters as well. Christian worship takes quite seriously the promise that God is "the praise of Israel" (Psalm 22:3).

Hearing a group of seminary students discuss a worship service they had attended, I was struck with their willingness to be bound by what they had been taught. They dissected and analyzed the "worship" service as coldly as bloodthirsty, New York critics feasting on a Broadway disaster. The wrong color paraments were used, the acolytes had been sloppy, the liturgist had failed to have the congregation stand for the gospel reading and the choir had chosen an anthem inappropriate for the church calendar.

"Did you sense the Lord there?" I asked them. "Was your heart touched?"

They stared at me in naked amazement, then exchanged fleeting glances, obviously embarrassed at my doddering ignorance. The service of which they spoke may well have been ugly and unengaging. This is certainly no defense of boring traditionalism.

Theater that is dull and stupid is no more or less spiritual worship than theater that is lively and talented. That, in fact, is the point. Worship is not theater at all, whether before an audience of gods or humans.

Why, Not How, To Worship

Now the question remains, if worship is such tender intimacy, why should we gather together in groups? Why not just stay in our prayer closets? Certainly we need those daily times alone with Jesus. We *must* have them. Yet there is also a great sense in which we need to be alone with Jesus in the company of others who are also alone with Jesus. In that way we share the intimacy both "vertically" and "horizontally."

I love all my children, and I love to be with them individually. I take a delight in them as individuals. Yet, I also love to sit down at dinner time and enter into fellowship with them all. I love to see them relate to each other in the presence of their parents. We laugh, love, share and enjoy each other. I believe there is an element of true worship in the family dinner hour.

In matters spiritual, it is so very easy to come up with the wrong answer, simply by asking the wrong question. Sensing the hand of God resting mightily upon him to whom she spoke, the "woman at the well" (John 4:20-24) determined to seek a fresh insight on a troublesome religious argument of her day. Her people, the Samaritans, held Mt. Gerizim as the abode of God on earth and the center of true worship. The Jews turned instead toward the temple at Jerusalem. Perhaps, she reasoned, this prophet might shed some new, albeit Jewish light, on the matter. The problem, of course, was that she asked the wrong question. Her last words in verse 20, "... where we must to worship," are in stark contrast to Jesus' last words in verse 21, "... worship the Father."

Jesus deftly shifted the weight of the conversation from superficial religiosity to penetrating spiritual truth. The question is not of "where," but of whom should men worship. As long as "where" is allowed to remain the central issue, no right answer at all is possible. The moment the reality of the Father's true character, nature and worshipfulness comes into focus, the question of where becomes simply irrelevant.

God may indeed be worshiped anywhere. He is no more or less accessible from Gerizim's venerated brow than from David's Jebusite citadel! The point was hardly wasted on the woman. Inclined no longer to debate, her question immediately became one of whom not where. "Who is Messiah?" she asked.

Even so, when we open ourselves to his marvelous guidance, the Spirit of Jesus can pilot us through the rocks and shoals of pin-headed superfluities upon which many have made shipwreck of their faith. Keeping our eyes on the beacon of "greater truth" we can avoid running aground on sectarianism.

When "*how*" to baptize, for example, upstages the rite itself, the peripheral reigns supreme. *When* to serve communion is more important than the means of grace itself *only* for the petty. *What* to sing and *how* to light the candles quickly become a hallmark of the religiously pretentious. Liturgical irrelevancies overshadow worship in the name of propriety only for those who have lost sight of the real question. Sects spring up like volunteer mushrooms in the dark, dank basement of so-called "truth." How sad when the well-intentioned cling tenaciously to some sacrosanct Gerizim of "worship" and miss the very presence, the person, the holy one—even Jesus, the Messiah.

Jesus recognized, of course, that the problem was not just a Samaritan one. His own people in Jerusalem labored under the bondage of a wretched, misbegotten "temple mentality." Hoping to substitute the trappings of worship for the missing glory, the Jews of his day had settled into form without truth.

How easy it is to accommodate to an unwholesome, counterproductive, even sinful slavery to some particular idea of how to "do worship correctly." Seminaries foist off on unsuspecting young theologues the most pedantic nonsense about colors, choirs and candlesticks. Creeds and choir robes do not worship make. Nothing, no matter how "correct" nor how beautiful, has any business in Christian worship unless it will truly aid those present in praise or proclamation. Many modern, mainline churches are literally choking to death on a lifeless, bound-up, uninspired "order of worship" that was carved in stone years ago.

Roadblocks to True Worship

The outmoded temple mentality will no longer satisfy starving congregations ready for true praise and supernatural power. It never really did. It just anesthetized them with sameness. Even if it means utterly scrapping some classical items of yesteryear, we must settle for nothing less than worship in truth and Spirit. He, the Lord himself, is the object of our worship. When we are not truly met by his Spirit we have not truly worshiped.

Everything done in a worship service falls into one of three categories:

1. It may be irrelevant, traditional filler.

2. It may draw our attention to ourselves. Under this general label are all those things which are "performance"-oriented. Also in this category are those more subtle aspects of humanism and sentimentality.

3. It may fasten our gaze on God, in Christ, to the explicit end that we express to him our praise and thanksgiving or that we hear from him.

Anything under category one should be summarily dropped.

Although this will vary from fellowship to fellowship, it is my personal observation that such "acts of praise" as responsive readings and the repetition of creeds are generally drop items. Nothing is worship that is mindlessly sung or hollowly repeated purely out of tradition.

It is for that very reason, that the leader seeking to weed out these not-so-sacred-cows of the services in a traditional church may encounter rugged resistance. The passionless, dull-eyed repetition of the Apostle's Creed or the uninspired chanting of the doxology require little serious involvement, do not engage the spirit and can be easily mumbled through without any sincere confession, repentance or faith. Hence, they become the comforting pacifiers of a child-like congregation eager to avoid any dynamic dialogue with a living God. To deprive such a congregation of its religious play-pretties may incite it to riot. There is no rage more immediate than that of a band of full-grown babies suddenly deprived of a well-worn teddy bear. The thought of anything actually being expected of them in a worship service is utterly infuriating because it threatens their complacent, self-conscious Sunday morning family adventure into the land of the Easter Bunny.

Certainly, we need substantive credal stands under our faith. Furthermore, this is not to say that all tradition is bad. It is to say that too much time is wasted trying educate congregations "up" to certain traditional acts of worship instead of being adventuresome enough to find fresh ways of teaching the doctrines of the faith in the context of powerful worship.

For a great, sad element of traditional Western "worshipers" the concept of entering the courts of a living God with intentional praise and thanksgiving is alien and even offensive. The very idea of actually hearing from the God through whose gates is rather like expecting to see little green men tumbling down the gangway of a flying saucer. Yet, by reclaiming the "dead air" of worship—by refusing to allow congregations the lethargic conceit of droning through prayers printed in bulletins and idiotic confessions of personal "shortcomings" and "national sins against the universe"—they are forced toward the reality of his presence. Expect reluctance, to say the least.

Everything in category two should be prayerfully inspected. This will tax the mature discernment of the worship leader. Very little is cut and dried here. Attitude, atmosphere and the witness of the Spirit are the keys instead of objective criteria.

Musical Pitfalls

Special music, for example, is a very powerful tool of worship. God can sometimes communicate through a sung message in a way not possible even through anointed teaching. Furthermore, excellence is to be striven for. Thank God we have moved past the era where the Lord's music was necessarily shabby and talentless. Yet, care must be exercised to guard against allowing the fleshliness of pride in performance to crowd out sincere, humble ministry.

Musicians and worship leaders whose special ministry is directed toward youth must be especially careful. "Christian rock" singers have gotten so defensive about the style of their music that they have often been totally insensitive to their own performance-oriented carnality. An argument with merit is that Scripture fails to single out one style of music as "Christian." While it is true that these musicians are sincerely hoping to meet young people where they are, they are too often being incautious with respect to subliminal communications.

Beat and rhythm aside, "Christian" lyrics fail to justify the blatant sensuality of immodest clothing or pelvic gyrations borrowed from the world. In the interests of meeting druggers where they are, shall we sink to soul-winning with a joint between our lips? Hardly! By the same token, a Christian musician hoping to reach a youth sub-culture saturated in sexual innuendo, hopelessly compromises the message if jeans are too tight and "dancing before the Lord" incites lust in the opposite sex.

"I dress as they do, to get them to listen," said one Christian singer. Granted, there is validity to the missionary concept of cultural identification. However, the question remains: why does the "youth" audience dress as it does? Imagine if you will an angry, rebellious teenaged boy sporting an earring only to infuriate his father, wearing yellow paint on his face because he hates himself as he is and carrying a switch-blade because he is seething with violent, anti-social bitterness. Does the sight of a "Christian" band wearing earrings, leopard-skin tights, painted faces and brandishing plastic machine guns with which to "shoot Satan," challenge that boy? Or do they only confirm him in his neurosis? Could it be that that boy's rebelliousness and anger go utterly unconfronted and his hurt unhealed because the band, lusting for his admiration, applause and perhaps money, refuse to run the risk of his rejection? Could it be that a fear of the scandal of the cross in the face of the teen sub-culture is only camouflaged by pious phrases like "meeting kids where they are?"

At another level the same yeast of fleshly performance may often spoil the loaf of church choir music. Self-important choir directors who see their goal in life as raising the cultural sights of the peasants in the pews have no place in worship. Endless, thousand-fold amens at the end of interminable formal, pastoral "prayers" intoned in King James English do *not* engage people in praise.

Good Worship Etiquette

A worship service must be *worship*, never *performance*. Granted, special music always has about it an element of performance. Even the excellence thereof must, at least by the profound intention of the heart, be *only* to give glory to the King.

Worship in the spirit is facilitated by music of praise which is simple. Hymns and hymn books can, at times, have a binding effect on a congregation. Hands filled with hymn books are not easily lifted in worship. It is often useful to mix familiar hymns with Scripture choruses. These choruses should be simple, melodic, easily learned and repeated enough times for the congregation to sing them without having to concentrate on the words. Praise songs should not draw attention to the songs but should rather allow the singers liberty to truly worship.

A worship service should not be long just for the sake of being long. Some charismatic congregations take truly sinful pride in worshiping longer than others. The worshipers must, however, feel an unhurried freedom to linger with Jesus. Periods of quiet praise should never be intimidating to the leader, nor should he draw them out until the congregation is made to feel awkward and uncertain. In an atmosphere of uncertainty, worshipers feel self-conscious and are less likely to concentrate on Christ.

This kind of balanced, Spirit-led worship leadership is infinitely taxing; it requires a high degree of sensitivity, humility and maturity. To combine authority, order and discipline with liberty and unhurried freedom of response to the Lord's presence is not child's play. Yet when it is learned, worked at and grown into, it is a beautiful and healing experience for all. The object is to give a fellowship the sense of order while affording folks liberty of expression. Some will raise their hands. Some may sway to the music or even dance to the livelier melodies. Some may sing in quiet adoration. Some may need sweet encouragement to try a bit more physical investment in praise, such as hand raising. Such encouragement, however, must never be arrogant, abrasive or condescending. The desire is to free people to worship not foster resentful resistance.

A balance in the music should be carefully sought. There ought not to be *only* driving, fast choruses for an hour. Singing *The Horse and Rider* followed by eight others of the same tempo will exhaust a congregation. Worse, however, it never gives time for that precious, contemplative sweetness necessary to deeper worship. We must not let "free" worship degenerate into infantile "campfire" songs. By the same token if every chorus sounds like *Alleluia*, many will miss the ebullience of spirit which also typifies the joy of the Lord.

The worship leader must pray for discernment to immediately check any sign of carnality. I clearly remember one charismatic church where the woman leading the music was so unseemly in dress and so arrogant in attitude that my spirit was vexed. I have been in far more traditional churches, however, where dozing congregations sat completely unengaged spiritually. The "worship" leader moved in his own universe; the parishoners sat emotionless in theirs, obeying because they did not know what else to do.

Face it, pagan performance and dullness alike are easier than mature, balanced worship in Spirit. Furthermore performance feeds our lust for applause, preeminence and prestige. There is in the heart of people that sinful pride which *wants* their priests better dressed, altars more beautiful and temples more luxurious than those of others. It was not Nimrod alone who built the Tower of Babel. He simply tapped into the prideful, religious heart of a people who wanted, by their own effort, to build a place of worship grand enough to reach to heaven. Their efforts ended in angry, earthbound disillusionment and the rupture of community.

At Pentecost the God of heaven inhabited the loving, humble praises of 120 people gathered for worship in a rented upstairs room. No one lit candles or formed a worship committee to get the "right" colors on the altar. They put their hearts on the altar instead of religious trappings. And in blazing glory, the curse of Babel was broken. Religious pride that vaunted itself toward heaven was stripped away. In the scandal of simple praise that remained, the church was met by its God.

CHAPTER XIII

The Virtue of Christ

❖

HEALING AND THE SPIRIT

As dust drifted down on his head, Jesus looked up. Surprisingly, shafts of light began to sprinkle through. As the roofing lifted away, four heads appeared, the sky behind them framed by the broken ceiling. Suddenly they disappeared and just as suddenly they were replaced by an amazing sight. A man, a dreadfully crippled man on a mat, was lowered into the room by ropes. Finally his twisted form rested on the floor at Jesus' feet.

A breathless silence hung heavily in the air. Every eye was on Jesus. The same question filled every mind. What would Jesus do? Would he heal the man on the stretcher?

Suddenly, softly, yet with unwavering authority, Jesus spoke to the poor wretch before him, "Friend, your sins are forgiven" (Luke 5:20).

Of all the responses Jesus might have made to that man's infirmity, no one in the room anticipated *that*. Had he said, "Stand up and walk," some would have expected it. "Your infirmity is

the will of God, go and learn patience," would have been no sur-
prise at all to many there. Even a denunciation of the man's sin,
for which his condition was a just a reward, would not have been
totally unexpected.

"Be of good comfort, son, your sins are forgiven," Jesus said.

Anger, doubt and suspicion filled the air. Had they been
more courageous, the Pharisees would have shouted
"blasphemy." They certainly thought it. Scoffers dismissed the
Master's words as "spiritual-sounding camouflage" for his inability to heal the paralytic. The men on the roof felt their hearts
sag. Nothing! They had come with such hopes, such faith and
now, nothing. Nothing had happened!

Yet something had happened. Beneath the very noses of the
Pharisees but beyond the vision of the onlookers, something
very marvelous had begun. By the Finger of God, Jesus had
reached into that pitiful young man's bosom and had done open
heart surgery. The Lord cut away the malignant tumor of guilt
and sin that would have blocked the flow of healing power. The
process—the great, glorious, kingdom work of healing—had
begun. It was such *inner* healing, unseen and undetected by the
onlookers, that the diagnosis was unanimous. Nothing had happened!

Then suddenly, just when their hopes seemed most cruelly
dashed, it happened. The Master spoke and the moment erupted
before their eyes. "Take your mat and go home." As if the years
of paralyzed torture had never been, the young man's twisted
limbs and gnarled joints unfurled like a flag in a breeze. In heart-
stopping pops and squeaks, ligaments tightened, joints snapped
into place and muscles, atrophied from many years disuse,
swelled to strength.

Suddenly the man stood! Just like that. Right before their
eyes. Carrying the couch that bore him, he began to walk out.
His shouts of praise were joined by racking sobs from the rooftop and a sudden explosion of noise and movement in the house.
Grown men wept at what they had seen. Legalists bickered over
what had *really* happened.

Yet the fact, the grand, beautiful fact of it was that he walked and right before their eyes! Jesus had healed again.

"Your sins are forgiven." That shocked them all!

They remain, in fact, shocking words, even in the face of a body of literature and teaching on healing, which seems to be growing daily. Those five words and the entire incident of Luke 5:18-26, open a marvelous window on Jesus' concept of his own healing ministry. The vista thus afforded us is in sharp contrast with much that is currently being taught on healing.

More Than Physical Healing

First, Jesus' point of orientation in the Luke 5 account is clear right from the start. The Master appears determined to minister to this poor man as God the Father says. Jesus refuses to be blinded by the obvious condition of physical distress. Certainly the Lord saw his physical infirmity. He wasn't blind. Just as certainly, the fact that the men on the roof were acting in great faith could not have been wasted on the Lord. Their boldness to interrupt his teaching was surely born of a profound conviction that Jesus could and would *make their friend walk*. I refuse to believe that they were even conscious of their friends "sinfulness." Their sensible faculties were totally arrested by the man's deep and obvious physical distress. We dare not romanticize the four men peering down through the gaping hole in the roof. They wanted Jesus to *make their friend able to walk*! That was the thrust of their faith.

Not untouched, I'm sure, by their good and passionate desires for their crippled friend, the Lord responded instead to the Spirit's direction. The men on the roof viewed healing in the limited perspective of a hope to see their friend walk. Jesus, however, was ministering in the power of the Finger of God. That power is the Holy Spirit of God, in other words, the Spirit of the very wholeness of God.

The man's compassionate friends merely wanted him to

walk. The compassionate Christ wanted him whole. Jesus' heart ached for the *whole* man. Not content to see him leave with straightened legs and a twisted soul, Jesus ministered wholeness to the whole man by the Spirit of wholeness. The holiness of I AM is his wholeness. The Finger of God, the Holy Spirit, is the Power by which Jesus healed. He did *not* just make lame people walk or the blind to see. With the law of perfect wholeness inscribed in his own inner man by the Finger of God, Jesus manifested healing in his every word and deed.

In other words, it is a mistake to see Jesus as dispensing miracles of physical healing to men and women whose spiritual brokenness he ignored. Filled with the Spirit of wholeness himself, Jesus constantly ministered in that power that others might be summoned into wholeness as well.

"Rise and be healed" was the easier part. Jesus did not fail to address the power of the kingdom within him to the man's physical affliction. He discerned, however, that the poor fellow was quite simply unable to receive or, more importantly perhaps, maintain a physical healing unless he were delivered from a crippling bondage of guilt and condemnation.

"Your sins are forgiven," was no other than healing. It was not even preliminary to healing. It was at the very heart of Christ's healing ministry. The Lord's ministry was, and is, to the whole individual—physical, spiritual and emotional.

A Time for Balance

Now this must not be understood as an attempt to spiritualize the miracles of Christ. Nothing of the sort! We must not get squeamish about the Master's ability to heal physically. We must likewise stretch our own faith to believe that the power to heal is present with the Church in Jesus' name even now. Theological reluctance to the ministry of physical healing is often, I believe, nothing but faithless disobedience to God's Word.

I find it remarkable that many who describe themselves as

"Bible-believing" or "fundamentalist" employ exactly the same kind of theological contortions in dealing with physical healing as do the dreaded "liberals" on such fundamentals as the resurrection or the virgin birth. Any commitment to biblical integrity demands that we cease this evasive "reading around" both the miracles of Jesus *and* passages such as James 5:14. Sick, hurting people do not want convoluted theological lectures. They want a church that will stretch its hands out to them in faith, believing.

At the same time, however, I find that most of these same folks do not expect a Church that is infallible, inerrant and all-powerful. In other words, they turn with longing in their eyes, to see if the Church really believes what it says. Even as they expect, with good reason, the Church to be Christ's presence in the world, they do not expect it to be his substitute. It has been absolutely liberating to me to discover that many of the people who approach the Church with a need for healing, have a better balance than the Church does. I find that when the sick turn to the Church they are thrilled with whatever touch of healing they do receive and rarely blame any failure on the Church. In fact, I believe they are likely to "blame" anyone, especially themselves, before the Church. We must, therefore, be careful not to callously trade on this tendency by inviting the sick to blame *themselves* when results are not immediate and obvious.

I believe it is often the shrill self-consciousness and over-inflated claims of the church, rather than a lack of faith among the sick, that impedes the flow of power. I was preaching in an open-air crusade in Accra, Ghana some years ago when an old woman suddenly stepped out of the crowd and started toward me. She was shouting praises to God and waving a handkerchief as she came forward. She reached her other hand towards me and I spontaneously extended one of mine. While I continued to preach she clutched my hand for a moment, then still waving her kerchief disappeared back into the crowd.

Later that night the odd little incident began to disturb me. I turned to the Lord, my heart burdened with questions. "What did that old woman expect from me? What should I have done? What did the onlookers think?"

It seemed to me that the Lord spoke to me, there in Africa, in a way that relates to much that is said and done in the healing ministry. As clearly as I could hear his voice, I thought he said, "My child, take your eyes off yourself. What do you care what the onlookers thought? And as for the old woman, she did not expect you to *do* anything. Do not worry that she was confused. Like the woman with the alabaster box she simply made a spontaneous gesture of love to my Word. She just wanted to touch Jesus, and you were all she could see."

The world is not demanding more of the Church than we can give. Many refuse to pray with the sick because they are absolutely terrified of the possibility of no visible results. This, however, betrays that they are too closely identified with the results anyway. We are called to pray in whatever faith we have, expecting that the healing Christ be released into the need as God directs.

Too Complacent About Suffering

The healing ministry of Jesus was magnificent in its simplicity. He did not teach on "Eight Ways to Receive Your Healing." He healed the sick. Instead of flagellating the faithless with iron-clad theological syllogisms, he touched the wounded with the Finger of God.

I see two equal and opposite errors in much of what is being said about the healing ministry of the Church. On one hand, I hear those who seem to say that because we cannot understand *all* there is to know about healing, we must avoid that work altogether. The idea here appears to be symptomatic of the same adolescent spirit that causes a young bride to say that because she might burn a dish or two in learning to cook, she won't try at all. Except, perhaps among the independently wealthy, that is a posture hardly affordable. After all, perhaps a few culinary disasters are the price of expertise. Such timidity is similarly too expensive for a hurting, wounded world, even though charlatans lurk and threaten on every side. We *must* roll up our sleeves and get in there and "burn a few pot roasts."

I have already made enough mistakes in the healing ministry to fill a book. I expect to make more. I have absolutely no faith in any minister who says he or she has *not*. Yet, we must be of sturdy enough stock to come through the embarrassments and disappointments, richer and wiser for the experience and not paralyzed by disillusionment and wounded pride.

Some, thus wounded, have retreated into a limpid sort of "para-evangelical fatalism." Immobilized by bad experiences or fearful of ever having them, they hide behind the will of God. "If God wants to heal, he will and if he doesn't, he won't. I cannot dare to even attempt to change his mind." When I hear such reasoning I always think of the Moslem taxi drivers in Nigeria who paint "As Allah Wills" on their cabs, drive like crazy men and blame all the accidents on the will of heaven.

In much the same way many who resist praying with the sick compound the error by comparing their reluctance to Jesus' prayer in Gethsemane, "Nevertheless, Lord, not my will, but Thine be done" (Luke 22:42, KJV). Similarly, they say, we must submit our wills to God in sickness.

Of course! Yet what *is* the will of God in the face of our shattered need? To pray, in my brokenness, "Thy will be done" is nothing short of a plea for wholeness, because that is the will of God. I look at my sin and cry, "Thy will be done." I believe his will is for my salvation, not my damnation. I finally confront my bent to sinning and pray in Gethsemane-brokenness, "Thy will be done." Is it not to be sanctified by the Spirit of wholeness?

I understand that a place must be reserved in theology for redemptive suffering. Even so, it absolutely must be remembered that any imbalance that tips the scale for an untoward emphasis on suffering is unwholesome. Certainly, that is not where the weight lies in Scripture. From God's self-revelation as Je-

hovah-Rappha, to the work of Jesus, to the miraculous ministry
of the Church in Acts, the greater burden of the Bible is on healing.

If suffering is so precious to God's heart as a redemptive
tool, then why, in all of the New Testament, is there not one account of someone touching the hem of Christ's robe and going
blind? Why didn't Jesus walk the roads of the Holy Land dispensing leprosy or crippling children by the word of his mouth?
No! Over and over again we read, "Virtue flowed out of him and
healed."

When the woman with the abnormal flow touched Jesus, the
fountain of his life stopped the fountain of her death. The very
virtue of God's wholeness was so fully revealed in him that his
words, his countenance, his touch constantly articulated the
good will of God toward man. Upon sensing the woman's draw
on this virtue, Jesus said, "Who touched me?"

It is the woman's response to being "found out" that is re-
vealing indeed. "Then the woman, knowing what had happened
to her, came and fell at his feet and, trembling with fear, told him
the whole the truth" (Mark 5:33). In other words, in fear and
trembling she confessed that not only had she touched a man, a
rabbi, in an unclean state, but that she had been healed by it. She
sneaked up behind Jesus and touched him as if to purloin a healing. Do you hear her? She says, "I'm sorry! Please forgive me!
I've been healed, and I don't know for sure if it was God's will."
Behold, however, the Master's response! "Daughter, your faith
has healed you. Go in peace and be freed from your suffering"
(v. 34).

God, Not Faith, Heals

I shall return to this point later on with regard to the place
of faith. Let me say here that, taken in context, I do not see the
Lord's emphasis to be on *faith* but on *whole*. In other words,
Jesus is comforting the woman as to the will of God by point-

ing out to her that the end of her reach for faith was wholeness not brokenness.

"Look," he seems to be saying, "you touched me in faith and you are whole. Doesn't that tell you something? You did not steal a healing from a passing power source. When you reached out for healing, you touched who God is in ME! Before, there was an Abraham, I AM. And I AM is wholeness."

Surely we believe this to be true. If it is not, how could any Christian practice medicine? We proceed on the assumption that a Holy God is on the side of wholeness. And it is a good clear, biblical assumption indeed. Hence no Christian nurse need agonize over whether she is administering penicillin to someone God is zapping with an infection. No Christian surgeon must wait and pray for the liberty to extract an appendix which is ready to rupture in the body of a sick 10 year old. For the doctor who operates believing he will alleviate the lad's suffering and extend his life, surgery is consistent with God's good will.

Shall the church do less? We ought to lay aside all the soul searching and endless agony to act in faith consistent with what we know to be true of God himself. God is whole and when we pray for wholeness for others we are very near his heart.

If you remember I said earlier in this chapter that there were *two* equal and opposite errors. One is to be paralyzed by a misplaced concern that we do not know all there is to know; therefore, we had best stay out of it and leave it to God. The other, and its equal, is the position that having accepted wholeness as God's will, now claims the how, when, where and what of it as man's business. The one leaves it totally to God. The other leaves him out of it.

There is an ironic element of arrogant humanism in much of the modern charismatic teaching on healing that places the emphasis on faith instead of an active God. I am confident that this, a well-intentioned reaction to the faithless, weak-sister approach to the promises of Scripture, is taken as a requirement by much of evangelical Christianity. It is, however, a dangerous over-correction.

Recently a prominent TV preacher said, "Jesus is through healing. God is through healing." He went on to refer to Jesus' response to the woman who touched the hem of his garment. "'Your faith has healed you,'" explained this preacher, "means that she was healed by her own faith."

"If you are praying for God to heal you," he summed up, "you are wasting your time. In the atonement, God has done all he's going to do. Now its up to you to use your faith."

I do not intend to get into what was and was not accomplished in the atonement. That is a subject for a book in itself. What I am speaking to here is what I perceive to be a dangerous theme in a great deal of contemporary teaching on healing. If the emphasis on faith is allowed to go unchecked to its logical conclusion, the result may well be a "Godless" theology of healing. I believe that some today are verging on espousing a kind of charismatic deism. That is to say they seem to teach that God set certain principles of healing in motion and now sits quietly by while men either do or do not act on them. Althizer said that God is dead and the evangelicals screamed. Now some of those who complained the loudest claim he is retired.

Unfortunately we have not always been careful enough with our vocabulary at this point. If we have not meant to speak of an inactive God watching men run the universe by virtue of gnostic mysteries, then we have certainly sounded like it. For the sake of integrity we must make it clear that *we pray* and *God acts*.

Our aim, of course, is to be the best instruments we can be. By holiness of heart and life, by constant prayer, by the Word, by faith, through love, we hope that the healing virtue of Christ will flow through us. Yet we dare not lose sight of the fact that it flows *through* us only, not *from* us. It is God himself who acts. Sometimes he heals through us. I know of times he has healed in *spite* of me.

Pet Heresies on Healing

He is the fountain of healing. An active God of miracles, not our theories, not even our faith, is the hope of those in need. Not only must faith be seen in its proper perspective but healing itself must be comprehended in its broadest implications. I see in Jesus' healing ministry that his methods and manner were consistent with his message. As he made people whole, he also ministered in a way most likely to be healing in itself. His approach seems to me to be humble, practical and expressive of his concern for the whole person. Look again at the man lowered through the rooftop. Hardly stopping short of physical healing, Jesus came to that point of ministry in a way most likely to touch the whole person. First, he forgave the man. I believe the predominant theme of Jesus' healing ministry to be love, not faith. The virtue that flowed from him was surely the power of perfect love. It is to that which people respond in faith.

Second, I see that Jesus was not afraid of variation in the pursuit of reality. Some I fear, are more preoccupied with reinforcing some pet theory or advancing a hidden agenda then with genuine concern for the sick themselves. As I read the gospel accounts Jesus comes across to me as caring nothing for his reputation nor for staking out his theological turf. I see him as being practical and *real* in his concern for the afflicted.

In Mark 8:22-25 Jesus prays for the healing of a blind man. Christ's first words to the man are a poignant portrait of the caring Christ. "Do you see anything?" Jesus wants a realistic appraisal of progress. That idea is very threatening to some in the healing ministry. Fearful of being negative or without faith, or perhaps powerless, they tend to shy away from the idea of asking the obvious, "Now, I've prayed for you. Do you sense any sign of progress?" Jesus cared more for the man's healing than for his reputation as a healer. Furthermore he gave not one thought to protecting his theology of faith. He just wanted to know if his prayer had effect. "I see people;" the man replied, "they look like trees walking around." In other words, "I have progress but the work is not complete."

I shudder to think of such an answer being offered in some modern healing services. I can just imagine the response from the platform. "If you don't have any more faith than that, you're not going to be healed! There's no use for me to pray for you if you aren't going to make a more positive confession than that. Repeat after me: "I can see perfectly." Keep saying that by faith. Jesus has healed you. Now you are going to lose it if you don't clean up your confession."

How pathetic the picture of that poor blind man as he might struggle to describe the progress to such insensitive ears! In the public ministries of some who constantly emphasize faith as the preeminent theme in healing, there is a distressing tone of arrogant condescension toward those they seem to feel are too faithless, ignorant or stupid to get healed. There is, likewise, no appreciation for either practicality or progress. The "name-it-and-claim-it" nonsense has very nearly gutted the contemporary Christian vocabulary. The thought of a modern Christian trying to respond "spiritually" to the Lord's simple practical question ("Do you see anything?"), is almost ludicrous. Yet we force it on each other.

Jesus did not seem given to such heartless bombast. His genuine, open, loving concern seemed to invite unguarded response. The blind man just answered. "I can see, but not perfectly."

The Lord's response? Simple! He prayed again. Neither rebuking the man's lack of faith nor allowing himself to come under condemnation because of imperfect results, he quietly proceeded to pray again.

What a comfort this is to me! If Jesus himself had need of importunity at times, how much more should I divest myself of the egotistical fragility which fixes blame when results seem less, or less immediate, than hoped for. I have prayed with people once and seen partial healings. I rejoice in those. I have prayed with others over a period of time and seen progressive levels of healing. I have seen immediate miracles. Many times I have prayed and seen no visible results. Even though it may not be a perceptible change, I still believe that something happens every time the church ministers in the name of Jesus.

More Sensitivity Needed

"You tell about people you pray for and they get healed," said the middle aged housewife angrily. "Why don't you tell about some people you prayed for and nothing happened?" Teaching, as I was at that particular moment, in a Baptist church always presents its own special challenges. When it comes to the Holy Spirit and healing in particular, the Baptists have, perhaps, not always been on the vanguard of the movement. However, even with her obvious huff over the subject matter, I thought it was a legitimate question. It is easy to fall into the trap of "only telling the good parts." Perhaps she was responding to some of that in me. I can also appreciate the wounds of folks who have prayed for healing for loved ones and seen little change. It must seem frustrating to hear glorious stories of miraculous healing for others.

I have experienced moments of absolute agony when praying for the sick. At times I wanted to see a miracle so badly I thought I would scream. It is impossible to describe the feelings in a minister's heart when sick people, patently unchanged, stare at you with accusing eyes. I remember praying for a blind child in West Africa once and seeing nothing. Oh, how I wanted to see that little girl healed! I stared at her little shoulders as they led her away and swore I would pray for the sick no more. In fact, I prayed for healing the next night, but for nearly two months I had a great test of faith in that ministry.

The minister too frail for such gut-wrenching moments is unsuited for the healing ministry. He or she will either reject it altogether or will hide behind spotlights and dogmatic sloganism.

I am still haunted by the memory of a particular charismatic conference at which I spoke. After delivering the standard "party line" sermon on "confessional faith" which has become all too predictable at such meetings, the other speaker calmly announced, "God hasn't called me to lay hands on the sick." At which he summarily left the auditorium. An hour and a half later my wife and I were still praying with the sick.

If the ministry of healing is going to be entered into with even a modicum of integrity, it must be done with sensitivity, love, tenderness for the hurting and a willingness to keep on learning even in the face of "failure." In addition to these, a lively faith that a God of holy love wills wholeness for humanity, must be informed by a genuine humility before his sovereignty.

Having said all this, however, I must return to the woman's question. "What about those for whom you prayed and nothing happened?"

The problem is that her question is not as simple as she thinks. I can list a thousand examples of people for whom I prayed and did not *see* anything happen. I also doubt the veracity of any minister who claims not to have such a list of his or her own.

Yet even so, I still cannot categorically state that "nothing happened." For example, look one more time at the man lowered into Jesus' presence. If he or the onlookers had been asked about results after Jesus' first statement, what would they have said? When Jesus said, "Your sins are forgiven," call that his first healing ministry to the man. The onlookers would surely have sworn that such a feeble effort showed no results. Yet to say that nothing happened is to deny the whole universe of spiritual activity. What happened was perhaps unseen but no less spectacular than the physical stage of healing that followed.

The wide variety of methods, levels and types of healings which I see encourage me in the position that the Finger of God is still ministering, as he did through Jesus' ministry, to address the hurts of people with the very creativity that made kumquats and California redwoods on the same day.

Some Unorthodox Healings

At an independent church in Arkansas a man came forward who had a detached retina. The pastor, Worth Gibson, and I prayed for him and his sight was restored instantly! I also recall an elderly woman at a church in Powder Springs, Georgia. Despite the strongest corrective lenses she was virtually blind. She could not recognize her own daughter at more than 10 feet. I prayed for her in seven stages. After each prayer we informally tested for improvement. I felt led to keep praying as long as we saw improvement. At the end of 35 minutes of prayer she could identify a vase of flowers at about 30 feet, *without* her glasses. She was able to count fingers at that same distance with her glasses on. At that point improvement stopped and we ceased praying. Yet the partial healing she received was thrilling.

At that same church I prayed for a little girl whose sight had faded until, even with glasses, she could no longer read any but the largest print. I saw no improvement whatsoever. Strangely, when my eight-year-old son prayed for her she was immediately able to read in my Bible without glasses. Her mother testified that this was a miracle.

Sometimes results are difficult to measure due to the nature of the affliction. High blood pressure, for example, does lend itself to immediate measurement. Over the years I have followed up on some such cases. In particular, I have been happy to see the enduring healing of a certain young girl in Waycross, Georgia. At the First United Methodist there, the pastor, Harold Tucker, and I prayed for a girl with epilepsy. In the moment I could not tell, of course, that anything happened. Yet she has never had another seizure.

Along with the local pastor, I prayed for the hearing of an elderly man in Kentucky. There was no improvement that night, but when he awakened in the morning he could hear a mockingbird singing outside his window for the first time in many years. Why the delay? I have no idea.

Having arrived early to a service at a Church of South India near Samariah, India, I had unhurried prayer with a mute girl of about 11. She could not utter one sound. S.E.A. Jesudason, the director of our Indian Missions, prayed with me for a few moments. Then we tested the girl. Her elder sister was quite excited that she could make even the weakest of sounds. After only 10 minutes or so of more prayer, the girl could say "thank you," "Father," "God," "Jesus" and several other words (in Tamil, of course). When she spoke into the microphone in the meeting that night people left the service immediately to collect the sick in their own families. We prayed with the sick until midnight.

My pastor, Lawrence Lockett, is a marvelous man of God. When the Lockett's new baby was born with rectal fistula the doctors felt that surgery was an unavoidable necessity. In a revival service at our church we prayed for that baby, and when they got to the parsonage that very night the baby was healed.

One of the most dramatic healings I ever witnessed happened at the Columbia Drive United Methodist Church in Atlanta, Georgia. The granddaughter of the pastor, Al Bruce, was desperately ill. Her digestive tract was not functioning properly and despite repeated hospitalization at Atlanta's famous Emory Hospital, the baby was failing rapidly. The night we prayed for little Joanna I honestly had to struggle for faith. Her appearance was so desperate that I was shocked. From that moment on the child improved, however, and over the next few years came to full health.

My own daughter, Rosemary, was born with no opening for the tear duct in one eye. It was not a major problem, of course, but would have required a minor surgical procedure. We prayed for her for some time in a more or less haphazard manner with no results. Finally we felt led to apply what Tommy Tyson calls "soaking prayers." Our entire family began to "soak" Rosemary in prayer. Grace at each meal, family altar, morning prayer and a dozen touches all through each day were administered. Every believing visitor to our home was asked to pray and friends and relatives were conscripted. For two weeks nothing happened. One morning we awakened for find a perfect opening for the tear duct and have had no trouble since. After which of those hundreds of prayers did nothing happen? Did she receive an instantaneous miracle after the last one or was it rather a process of faith, love and importunity?

More Unusual Healings

An interesting portrait of the healing process was shown to me in the life of my dear friend, Kenneth Hewitt. I saw, in the last few years of his life, a marvelous insight into God's concern with healing as a process of life toward ultimate wholeness.

While separated from his wife and living in serious sin, Ken was converted to Christ. A short time later, several others and I prayed for Ken to receive Holy Spirit baptism. From the brokenness of destructive relationships to holiness and a precious boldness in soul-winning, we all watched Ken blossom in the healing process. When Ken and his wife, Joyce, remarried, the manifest reality of the Finger of God at work in his and their lives was gloriously obvious to even unbelievers.

In their town of Moultrie, Georgia, there are literally dozens of men whose testimonies include reference to Ken Hewitt. When Ken was diagnosed as having cancer, hundreds began to pray for healing. Several years later Ken died. In those years, however, God gave Ken a wholesomeness and vitality that made it virtually impossible to believe the cancer was still there. The doctors were amazed at the lack of pain Ken suffered even at the last. Astonishingly, with massive malignancy in his digestive tract, Ken ate and digested food within hours of his death!

One marvel of God's healing power in Ken was the literal radiance of his life and countenance to the very end. From a bed rolled onto a stage Ken spoke to 1,600 men of the love and faithfulness of Jesus the last night before he died. At his funeral five people accepted Christ in a service so filled with joy and triumph that one older lady told me, "This is the strangest funeral I ever saw. It's happier than some weddings I've been to."

The greatest part of all is that in the process of bringing Ken from brokenness to wholeness, God's love through Ken touched so many others. I simply cannot see any way in which Ken's years as a Christian were anything except a healing miracle. On his deathbed with cancer, Ken was more "whole" than the broken, shattered, burned-out husk of a "healthy" sinner he had been just a few years before.

The glorious final reality, of course, is that *now* Ken is enjoying the radiant manifestation of that healing process! Now in heaven and in his glorified body, Ken knows what we see in a glass darkly. Death for a Christian is not the splintering finality of the process of dying. For the born-again, death is ultimate healing. It is the great moment of shedding off the last dusty rags of mortality to burst fully alive and utterly whole into the presence of the King.

In San Jose, Costa Rica, Methodist Bishop Roberto Diaz, former Bishop Fernando Paloma and an American pastor from New Mexico, Ted Grout, joined me in praying for a little boy named Pablo. One of his legs was shriveled, twisted and as much as three inches shorter than the other. He walked with the help of a brace and only then with an awkward lurch.

As we prayed I held his ankles in my hands with the soles of his shoes against my chest. After only a few seconds of prayer the leg actually twisted in my hand and extended itself. When Rev. Grout helped me measure, we saw that it was still not quite right. After only a couple minutes more in prayer we tested again. It appeared exact. We removed the brace and both shoes. When Pablo walked as evenly as an athlete it absolutely electrified the church. That very night his mother gave her life to Christ and was born again.

When I asked her if she wanted to give her life to Christ, she answered me, of course, in Spanish. Through his tears Rev. Ted Grout translated for me, "How can I not?" She said. "Tonight I have seen him."

Jesus ministered wholeness by the Finger of God everywhere he walked and in each word he spoke. The healing virtue flowed even from the hem of his garment. The poor, lonely, broken, doomed, damned world turns its lonely eyes to the Church hoping for just what Pablo's mother saw—a glimpse of Jesus.

CHAPTER XIV

Palaces Forsaken

❖

THE POWER OF EVANGELISM

*T*he lights of Lima were beginning to melt into the cloudy darkness beneath the huge plane when the dark-eyed young businessman seated next to me struck up a conversation. I was on my way back to the United States from an evangelistic mission and he was returning from a government agricultural conference.

When I explained that I was a preacher, he was immediately eager to talk. In fact, his enthusiasm was a bit disarming. He leaned close, speaking in a warm conspiratorial tone.

"I have just been filled with the Holy Spirit!" he said. "Do you know what I mean?"

"Oh, yes," I said. "I received the Holy Spirit in 1975. Isn't it wonderful?"

"You know," he said, "sometimes friends would try to talk to me about the Holy Spirit. I would always tell them to just win people to Jesus and leave this Holy Spirit thing alone. But the thing was I never did actually win very many. I talked about evangelism. I served on the evangelism committee at my church, but all we did was plan the revival each year. The preacher won the lost, and I was in favor of it. Since I received the baptism in the Spirit *I* have actually been winning the lost. It's amazing!"

"Did you come under conviction about soul winning through a sermon or book or what?" I asked.

"No, no," he said. "That's what I'm trying to say. I didn't come under conviction about it at all. It just began. I used to talk about it, and now I *do* it! What I had dreaded and avoided before is suddenly as *natural as breathing.*"

That phrase, *as natural as breathing*, is actually more theologically appropriate than he probably dreamed. The Holy Spirit is indeed the breath of God, and as believers breathe deeply, the work of evangelism comes alive. No longer a dreaded duty born of evangelical conviction, soul winning follows empowerment by the Holy Spirit as naturally as light follows the flipping of a switch. As the young businessman said, that which is loudly affirmed as right and good in the evangelical church is often left for the preacher to actually *do*. It would be difficult, in fact, in the evangelical community to find a "no" vote on evangelism as a priority.

Whistling Past the Graveyard

Despite this agreement, however, many churches (and whole denominations) are barely treading water, let alone gaining members or saving the lost.

The United Methodist Church, of which I am a member, began 1969 with approximately 10.8 million members. The potential harvest for Christ and the kingdom through such an army is mind-boggling. Yet in the next four years we United Methodists lost virtually three-quarters of a million members—a number greater than the entire population of North Dakota! What was our answer? At the General Conference (Methodism's quadrennial denominational assembly) we approved evangelism as the major quadrennial emphasis by a huge majority.

Yet since 1976 we have been losing about 65,000 members a year.

We are standing like a doomed Dutch boy with our collective finger in a hole that is rapidly threatening to explode. In 1984, the General Conference voted (notice *voted*) to double the denomination by 1992. If that had not been so sad, it would have been laughable. Imagine a group of wounded soldiers lying on the battlefield. Their life-blood oozes into the mud where they have fallen. Their ammunition exhausted, their comrades in a rout and their officers in confusion, they now *vote* to win the war. Just such ghoulish absurdities will continue to haunt America's ecclesiastical conventions until we categorically refuse to attempt ministry, *especially* evangelism, without a fresh outpouring of the Holy Ghost.

It is utterly impossible to vote a revival into existence. To continue to approve membership increases by acclamation while thousands disappear annually is whistling past the graveyard. We must return with broken hearts to Jerusalem, confess our need and poverty and cry out to God for an anointing of the Holy Spirit. Len Ravenhill said, "There will be no revival as long as men are content to live without it." Until we get desperate enough to drop the hurry-scurry of the modern church, forsake the asinine political pronouncements of the college of bishops and get back to Pentecost we continue to flirt with denominational suicide.

The trailer parks, ghettos and "swinging singles" apartment complexes seethe in contemptuous disrespect for the complacent middle-class church busily tidying up after its covered-dish suppers and turning blind eyes to those living and dying in sin across the street. There will be no serious storm of persecution to burst on the church in America until we aggressively, energetically begin to reclaim the territory we blithely conceded to Satan in the past. Hitler did not hate Neville Chamberlin. Hitler laughed at him! He mocked the British Prime Minister for the fuzzy-headed old maid he was, muttering mealy-mouthed platitudes about peace while benignly consigning to darkness and slavery the weeping multitudes of the Rhineland.

Satan *and* those he enslaves laugh at a church so absorbed with itself that it has no concern for the lost and so dignified that it refuses to dirty its hands in the sooty business of "plucking brands from the fire." The modern Church encounters little resistance from the enemy because she seems to have decided to let sleeping dogs lie. As long as we launch no beachheads on enemy territory, Satan will be happy to let us twiddle our thumbs and play church. Cut-glass cathedrals filled with successful suburbanites are absolutely no threat to the kingdom of darkness— as long as they stay where they are.

Real, Live, Pentecostal Evangelism

From the Upper Room the 120 marched into the streets of Jerusalem like God's storm troopers. They served notice on hell that henceforth no place was safe from the name of Jesus. It was obvious immediately that they intended to fill the whole city, indeed the whole world, with their doctrine. Still hot from the blast furnace of Pentecost, they melted the stony hearts of an antagonistic mob that had, only a few days earlier, screamed, "Crucify him!"

The deciding difference in evangelism is neither motive nor method. It is Pentecostal power. One congregation sits in a muddle, studying the results of a community survey done by hired "experts," while another within blocks of it seems to explode in spontaneous revival. A mainline Protestant downtown "First Church," its membership gradually hemorrhaging, languishes in self-pity because its community is changing. The great empty hulk of its Southern Gothic sanctuary testifies sadly that its glory days are gone in the move to the suburbs. The diminishing congregation has become a gradually graying knot of sad Sunday-morning commuters, and its pulpit, no longer a plum, is a political sand-trap deftly dodged by the slick young corporate climbers.

Three streets nearer the ghetto, a vacant A & P rocks with the praises of 800 exuberant but poor blacks and whites who have forgotten what color they are.

God's plan for evangelism will never be fully comprehended by tidy seminars on church growth techniques. Nor will the work be finally fueled by fiery exhortations. Those may help to equip or motivate the saints, but neither will empower them. The compilation of community data may perhaps facilitate program, but it will not substitute for Pentecost. If by "church growth" we mean rescuing the perishing from death and hell, we will quickly confront the absolute inability of any human vehicle, regardless of how equipped it is.

Only supernatural Holy Ghost power can break Satan's bondage, penetrate with conviction the walls of souls calloused by sin, witness with the blood and cause faith to arise. That may be just as well accomplished in a store front as a cathedral and by blacks as well as whites. The true Pentecostal power for evangelism awaits no ordination, requires no education and knows no limitation. Its spontaneity defies the program-mongers. It's liberty contradicts all sectarianism and its direct, bold-faced simplicity confounds muddle-headed theologians.

Far from the sunshine evangelicals of today, the 120 sought no approval from the upper crust and took no votes for denominational growth. Much of what is called "evangelism" or "church growth" is nothing more than accident of demographics. Evangelism awards decorate the walls of some suburban churches which have done no more than hold a pail to the feet of bleeding inner city churches. Chasing suburban growth patterns, they abandon the cities to Satan.

They have "evangelized" the suburbs by making church membership easy and fun, substituting athletics for serious discipleship and watering down the gospel until heathen yuppies find it quite easy to "kick against the goads." Their growth is an affront to any serious biblical understanding of evangelism. Making their worship services positive and their sermons more upbeat, they construct buildings carefully designed to appeal to the tastes of their clientele. Populating pews with the unsaved and unsanctified while feeding them the lotus blossom gospel of pop-psychology and church league soft-ball may win denominational awards, but it is *not* evangelism. That holy work awaits a genuine move of the Spirit received from God by a repentant church on its knees.

On the very day the Holy Spirit baptized the Church in the Upper Room, three thousand repented, believed, entered in and continued! Moody said, "When the preacher is on fire, the people will come just to watch him burn." The same is true of lay people, congregations and entire denominations. Fear, wonder, awe, conviction, conversion, repentance, prayer, wonders, signs—these are the vocabulary of Acts 2:37-46. These are the signs of the Holy Ghost and the trail leads in irresistible power to Acts 2:47. That verse contains a 13-word-Holy-Ghost-Church-Growth Seminar. "And the Lord added to their number *daily* those who were being saved."

'The Lord Added . . .'

That thousands were added absolutely tantalized the numbers-conscious. That the *Lord* added is, however, the sobering reality that must *never* be forgotten. The Holy Spirit is the true evangelist. He is actively involved long before the preacher or soul winner arrives on the scene. The "foolishness of preaching" is certainly God's chosen means. The marvelous mystery of it is that in such foolishness the Holy Spirit moves somehow to do a work in the inner-most chambers of the hearer's heart. When the church attempts adding to itself, the effort eventually takes on a fake man-made flavor with a lingering aftertaste of flesh. Such "microwave" evangelism simply cannot replenish our ravaged ranks. When, however, paltry human effort and fleshy striving resign the field to the Holy Spirit, God will gladly add to his church. Isaiah 32:14-17 explains it perfectly.

The fortress will be abandoned, the noisy city

deserted; citadel and watchtower will become a wasteland forever, the delight of donkeys, a pasture for flocks, till the Spirit is poured upon us from on high, and the desert becomes a fertile field, and the fertile field seems like a forest. Justice will dwell in the desert and righteousness live in the fertile field. The fruit of righteousness will be peace; the effect of righteousness will be quiteness and confidence forever.

Churches that have become abandoned fortresses—or as the King James so eloquently puts it, "forsaken palaces"—can produce again. The deserted ruins of yesterday's crystal cathedrals *can* become high-yield vineyards once again. It will never be forced by ecclesiastical workaholics striving in the arm of flesh. When men do the adding, the real work is dealing with the ulcers and burn-out in the parsonage. The "work" of the church flowing in God's power is "peace."

'To The Church . . .'

Biblical evangelism requires a church-view informed by catholicity of Spirit so fierce that it affords very little latitude for petty parochialism. Nowhere in Scripture is there the admonition to "go into all the world and make Baptists of all men." Not least among the works of the Holy Spirit is his stretching of horizons. Exodus 2:21 says, "Moses agreed to stay with the man." Happily satisfied with home and hearth at Zipporah's side, Moses settled into a prosperous partnership with Jethro. Yet when the Finger of God tore away the blinders of fear and complacency, Moses' heart was touched by God's burden for the slaves in Egypt. It is the Holy Spirit that grants a broader world view and a truer church concept. It is by the Holy Spirit that pastors are called to foreign missions, professors to evangelism and construction workers to pastoring. It is also by the Holy Spirit—and it is no mean miracle—that selfish absorption with denominational priorities yields to an understanding of the Church as the catholic body of Christ.

Evangelism dragging the ball and chain of vested denominational interests will scarcely know liberty of Spirit. If the body prospers in any of its extremities, the other limbs, knowing their common bond ought to rejoice. Often, however, the denominationalists have lost all delight in seeing the lost saved because of their agony that a soul newly won might "join some other church." *What* other church? There is only one. I have often wondered what would happen if the Angel of the Lord appeared to the pastor at First Methodist one night and posed the following dilemma: "You may choose which of two great miracles you want. You may win 1,000 lost sinners to Jesus Christ, and they will join your church. Or you may win 5,000 lost sinners to Jesus Christ, and they will join the Assemblies of God." What fearful agony of soul might such a proposition foster for the poor pastor debauched by denominationalism. Would he, rejoicing in the privilege to enlarge the kingdom anywhere, choose the greater blessing for the greater good? Only by the power of the Spirit! And only if he sees himself as part of the whole body of Christ.

One phrase which seems to have taken root in the modern American religious vocabulary is, "parachurch organization." It is, however, a phrase which makes absolutely no sense whatsoever. It, furthermore, betrays our silly fascination with denominationalism. An organization cannot be parachurch anymore than a human being can be paraperson. Either it is part of the body of Christ or it isn't. Perhaps a more appropriate phrase is paradenominational. But then that would be a frank admission of an oft-denied but secretly held view that James Robison, for example is not quite as much in "the Church" as is the pastor at First Presbyterian.

In my own denomination there is a particularly noxious "more-Methodist-than-thou" syndrome which is sinful as well as counterproductive. I often fear that we shall only succeed in banging the Methodist drum so loudly that we drive the poor frightened heathens even deeper into the jungle. I am absolutely persuaded that if we but concentrate our efforts on winning the lost to Jesus, enough of them will drop into our own particular slots to satisfy even the heartiest appetite for church growth. If, on the other hand, we subtly substitute denominational growth for true evangelism, we shall find ourselves knee-deep in glorified Kiwanis Club membership drives. "God added daily to the church, his Church!"

There is nothing wrong with programs for evangelism. We must be practical and energetic in the holy work of winning the lost. Yet we must guard against allowing ourselves to think of evangelism *only* in terms of program. The "program-mentality" sets up a committee on evangelism and puts the matter in their hands. That mind set periodically "votes in" evangelism as a denominational emphasis. That is like the American Medical Association officially going on record that "breathing is beneficial to the human body." Evangelism is *not* just another program of the church. Evangelism is the day-to-day result of the indwelling power of God's Spirit at work in and through his Church. Evangelism is the reason for the Church. Evangelism is work, joy, burden and blessing of the Church . . . daily.

' . . . *Such As Should Be Saved*'

In a paranoid attempt not to offend contemporary society with our words, we have gutted the classic vocabulary of biblical evangelism. In some circles, winning the lost has been altogether replaced with rent strikes and soup kitchens. Work to improve the lot of the poor and oppressed is both biblical and evangelical imperative—just as church membership and good churchmanship are to be encouraged and practiced eagerly for growth and service.

We must, however, never allow ourselves to be intimidated about plain old, bold-faced, up front, *soul* winning! Loose talk about evangelism breeds disregard for the necessity of being born again. If evangelism means everything, it means nothing.

The primitive Church, on fire with the Spirit of Jesus, proclaimed the unadulterated gospel of Jesus Christ in power and saw thousands saved. Hence the evangelistic proclamation of the Pentecostal church was clear, concise and convicting. "Repent and believe!"

When the Holy Spirit baptizes a pastor, a congregation or a denomination, he descends like a consuming fire to burn away the fog of worldly wisdom that cloaks the naked simplicity of salvation by grace through faith. It is the Spirit of love who fills the heart of the church with a burning, aching passion to see the thousands of lost brought in. It is by the Spirit of power that preaching becomes a miracle. It is by the Spirit of faith that the hearts of hearers are pricked at the name of Jesus, that they find a witness with the blood and that they believe unto salvation.

A Methodist district superintendent told me that the "old-time tactics of calling people down front and all that, just won't work anymore." He was perhaps considering the sophistication of our age, the dullness of the modern spiritual jade or maybe the powerlessness of much contemporary preaching.

He had, however, failed to realize that it was in no less adverse conditions that a ragged little band of believers freshly filled with the Power of God saw thousands saved in a single day. The D.S. had failed, as so many do, to reckon on the Finger of God.

One night after I had preached an open air crusade in Tamale, Ghana, I was counseling with those who answered the altar call. Some 60 or so had come to the platform and prayed to accept Christ as Lord and Savior. I had led them as well in a prayer of renunciation, denying all ancestral gods and Mohammed. At the close of the prayer I gave them a brief exhortation on the efficacy of the blood.

"Now," I explained, "your sins are forgiven—completely! Everything you have ever done is forgiven, and you are born again. You are a child of God. Born again! If you died right now you would be in heaven with Jesus."

Suddenly from the rear of the seekers at the platform's edge, a man began to wave his arms as if to catch my attention. His eyes ablaze with hope and his countenance transfixed, he shouted, "Even me, white man? Even me?"

"Yes, my brother." I said, "Even the likes of you and me."

At his weeping and shouting the joy of the Lord swept over us all. The Finger of God had touched him. I wish that the Methodist district superintendent could have witnessed it.